ANIMALS IN THE NEIGHBORHOOD

AMERICAN RED SQUIRREL

Though their primary diet is pine and spruce cones, they also eat mushrooms, buds and flowers, and even bird eggs.

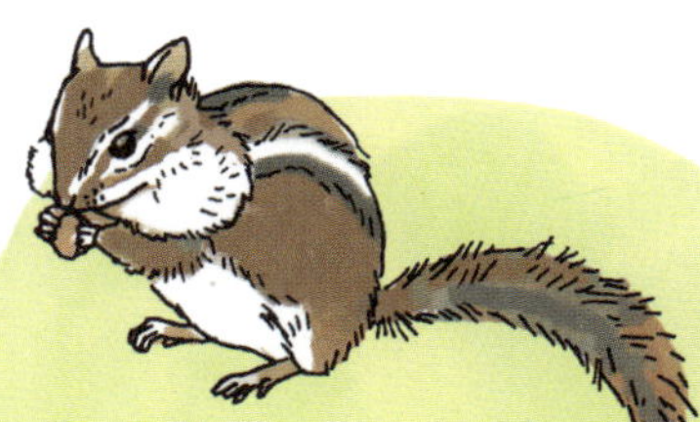

STRIPED SKUNK

This nocturnal omnivore's primary predator, the great horned owl, lacks a sense of smell.

WOODCHUCK

Woodchucks (or groundhogs) can climb trees if they need to escape.

RACCOON

Raccoons have 5 fingers but no thumbs on their highly sensitive paws. They are excellent swimmers.

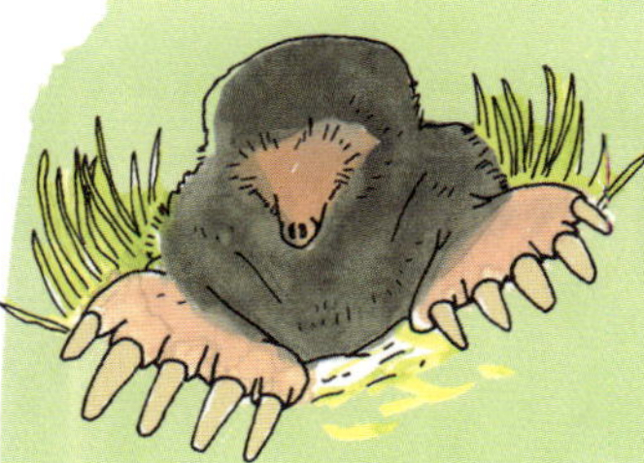

EASTERN CHIPMUNK

Chipmunks pack their food into their expandable cheek pouches and carry it back to their lair.

EASTERN MOLE

These solitary underground creatures eat worms and grubs. Though nearly blind, they have acute hearing.

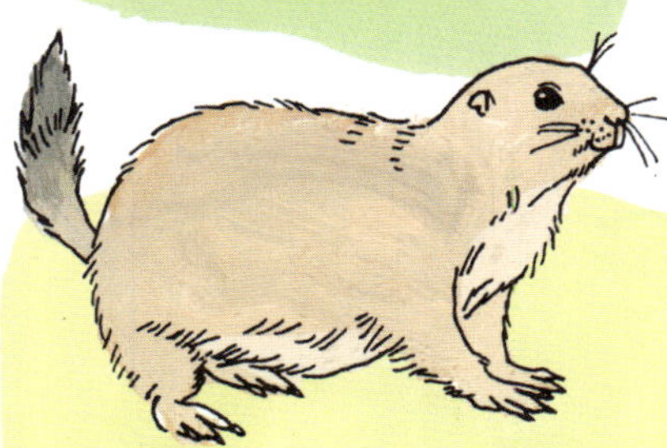

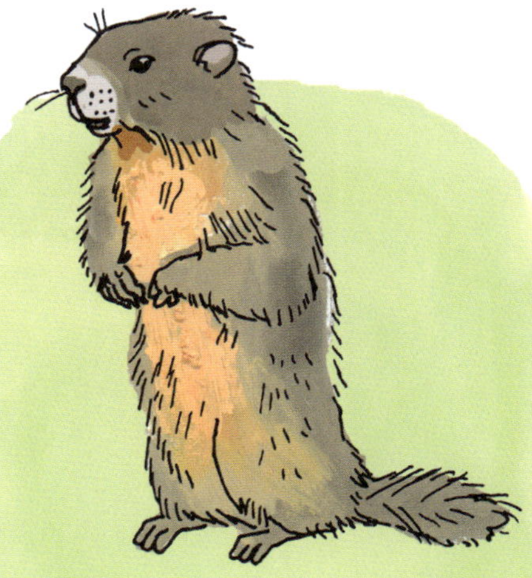

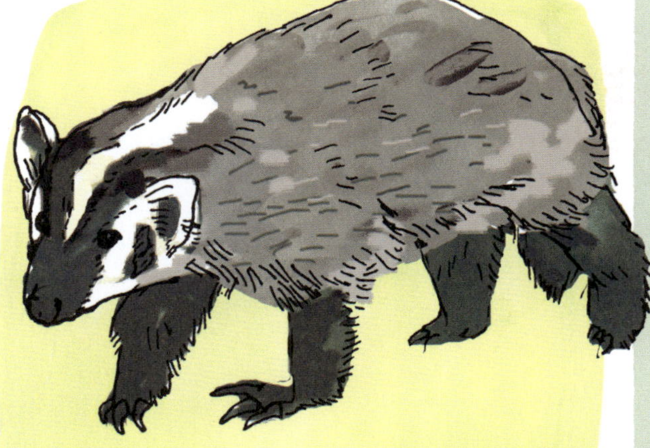

AMERICAN BADGER

Badgers are such strong burrowers that they can dig themselves into underground hiding within moments of any threat.

BLACK-TAILED PRAIRIE DOG

These extremely social animals live in elaborate underground "towns."

YELLOW-BELLIED MARMOT

Rather than dig burrows, marmots live in rocky piles in mountainous areas.

ANATOMY OF A BEE

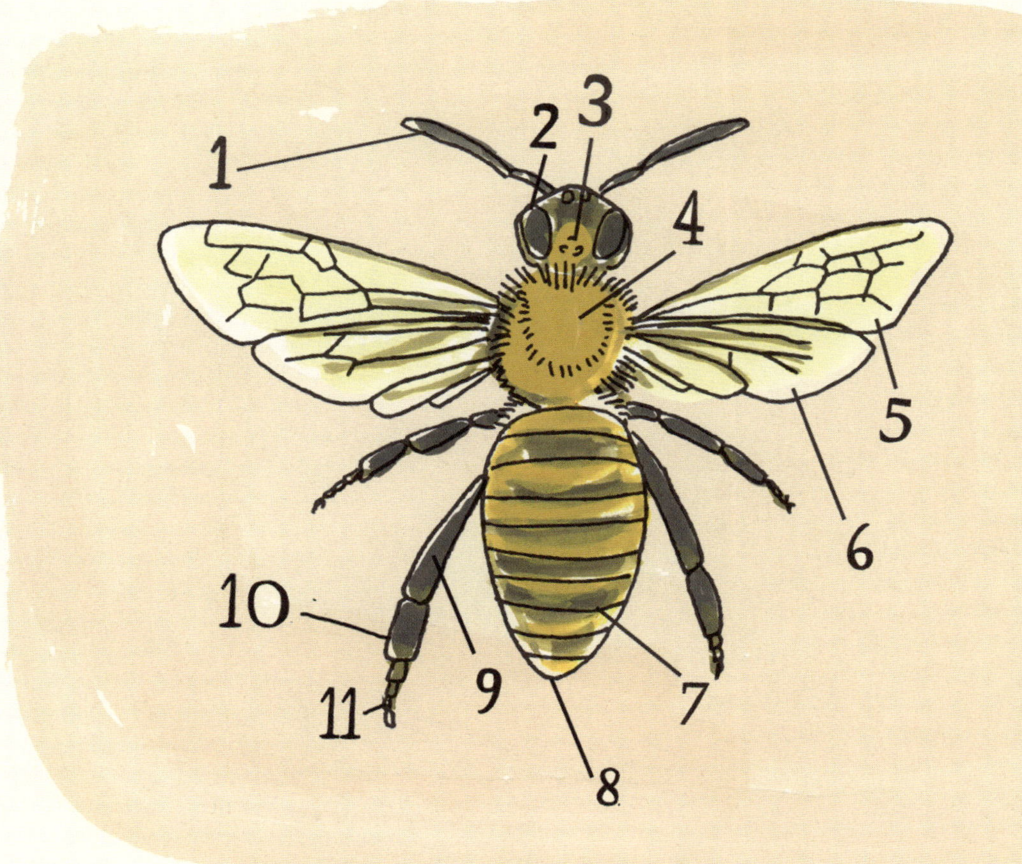

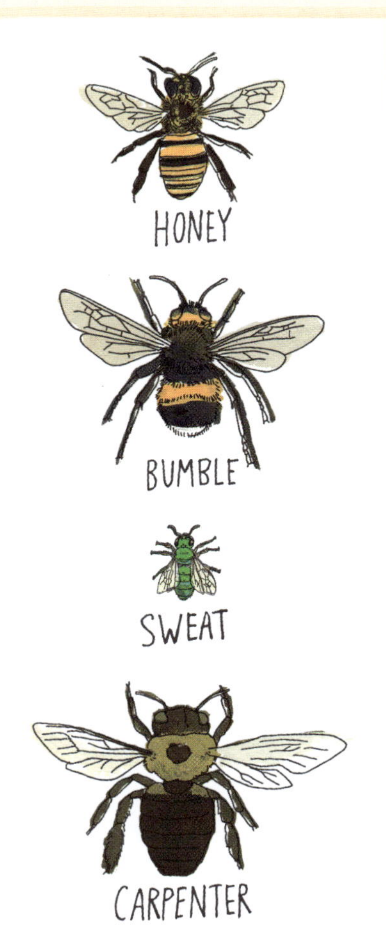

1. **antenna** - contains thousands of tiny sensors that detect smell
2. **compound eye** - for general distance sight
3. **ocellus** - three simple eyes used for low light conditions in the hive
4. **thorax** - segment between head and abdomen where wings attach
5. **forewing**
6. **hindwing** — 2-part wings hook together in flight but separate at rest
7. **abdomen** - contains all the organs, wax glands, and stinger
8. **stinger** - only present on worker and queen bees
9. **femur**
10. **tibia**
11. **tarsal claw** — three pairs of legs with six segments each; used for walking and packing pollen

BIRD BEAKS

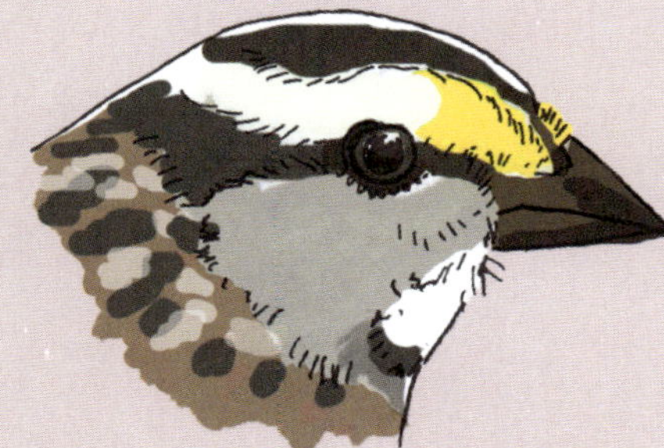

WHITE-THROATED SPARROW : great for crushing seeds and picking at bark to uncover hiding insects

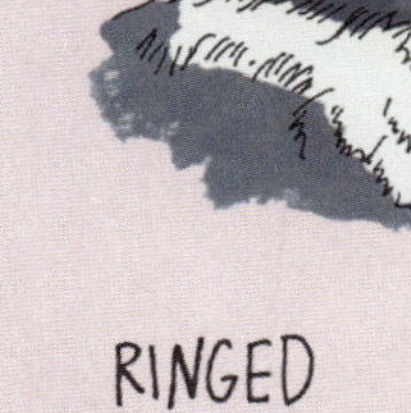

RINGED KINGFISHER : wedge shape creates no splash when entering the water

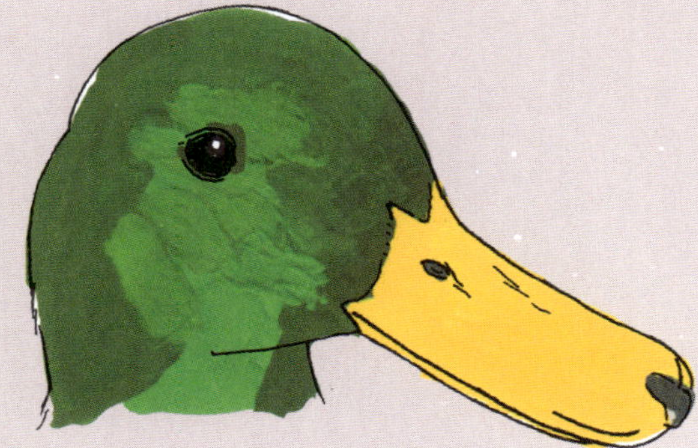

MALLARD : used for skimming in shallow waters

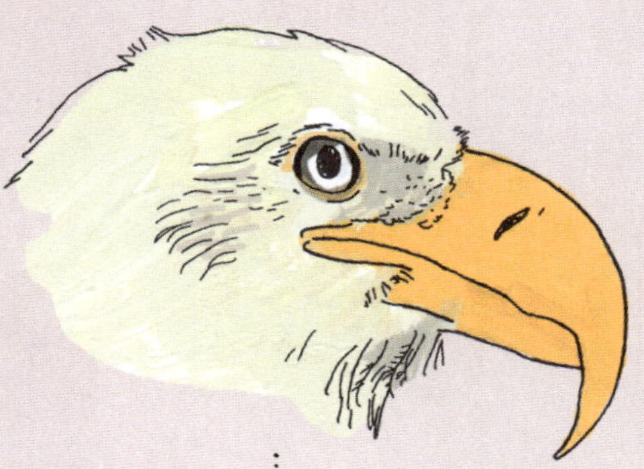

BALD EAGLE : hooked for tearing up prey

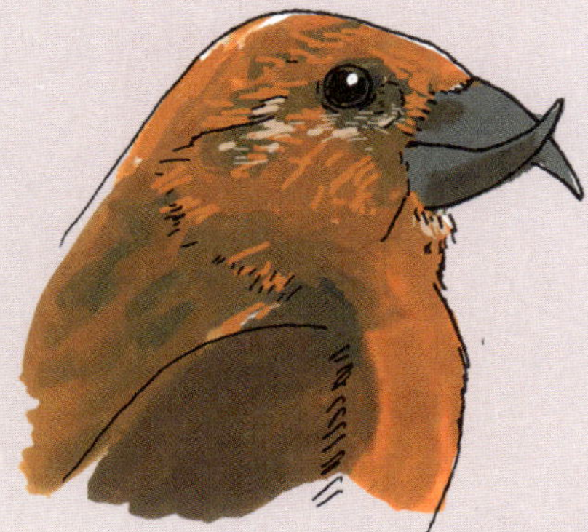

RED CROSSBILL : helps with prying apart scales of a pine cone

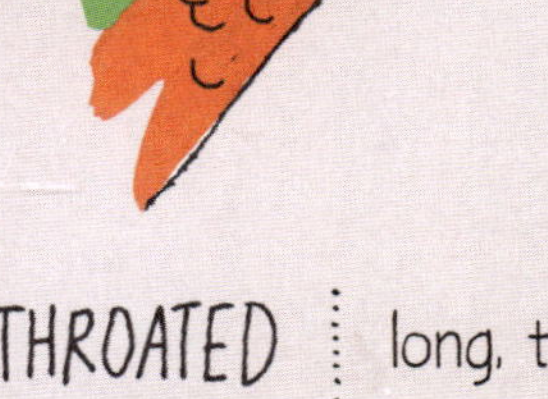

RUBY-THROATED HUMMINGBIRD : long, to probe into flowers

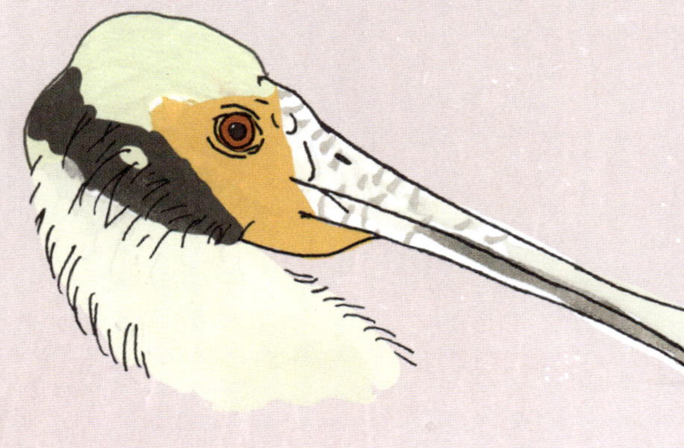

SPOONBILL : partly open bill sweeps through water to find prey, then snaps shut to capture it

BIRD NESTS

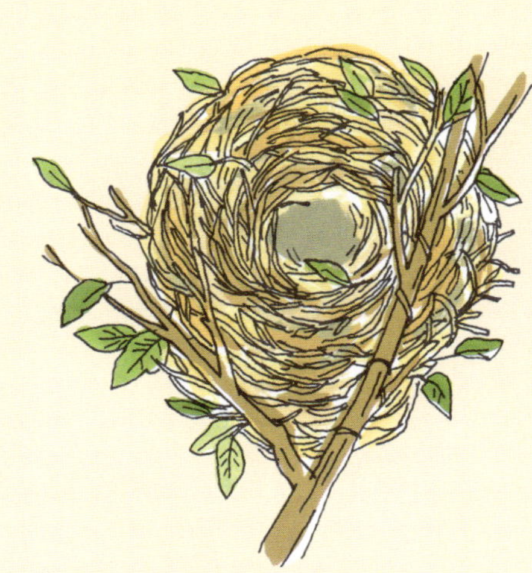

House Wren

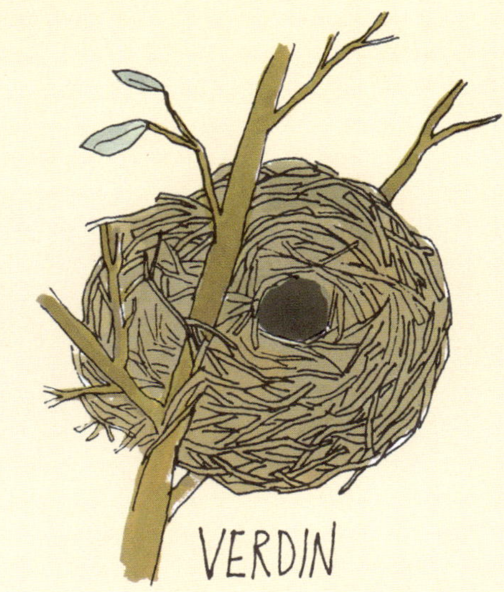

Verdin

Snowy Egret

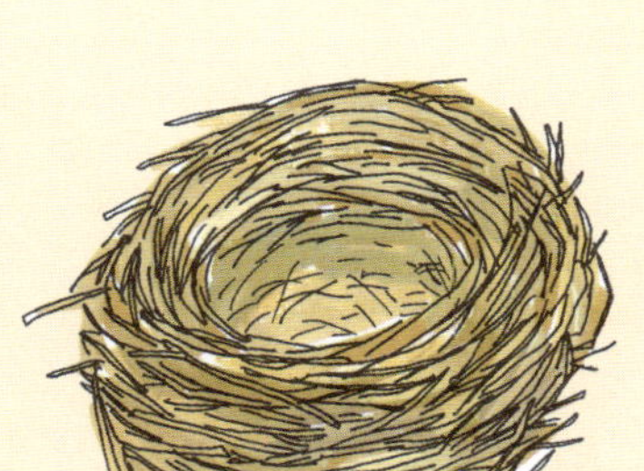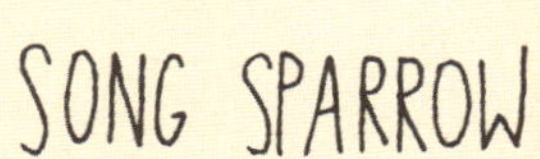

Song Sparrow

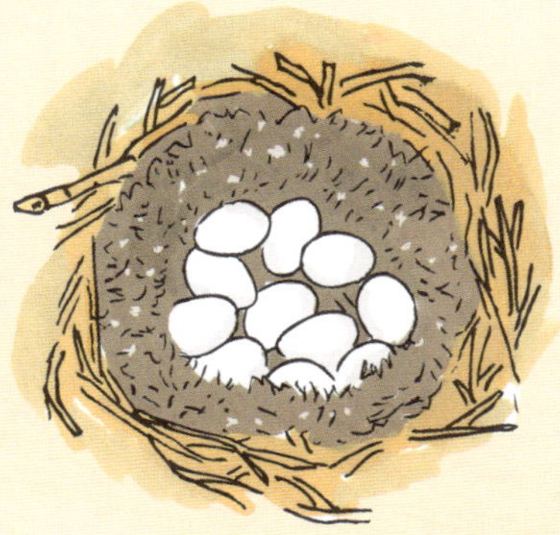

Mallard

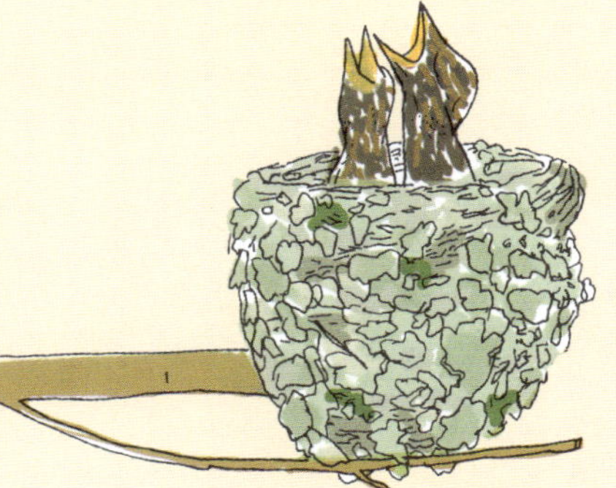

Anna's Hummingbird

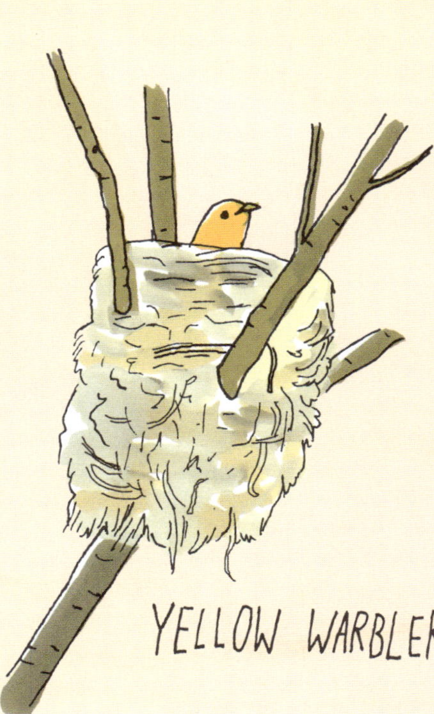

Yellow Warbler

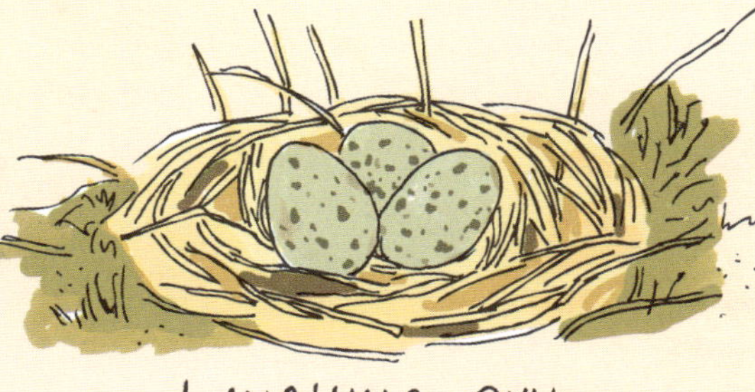

Laughing Gull

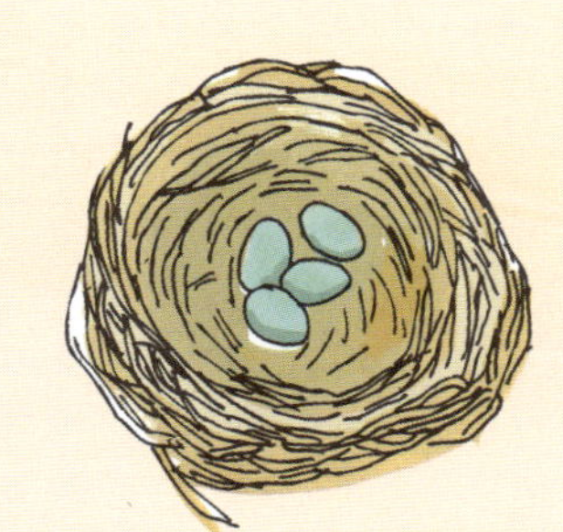

American Robin

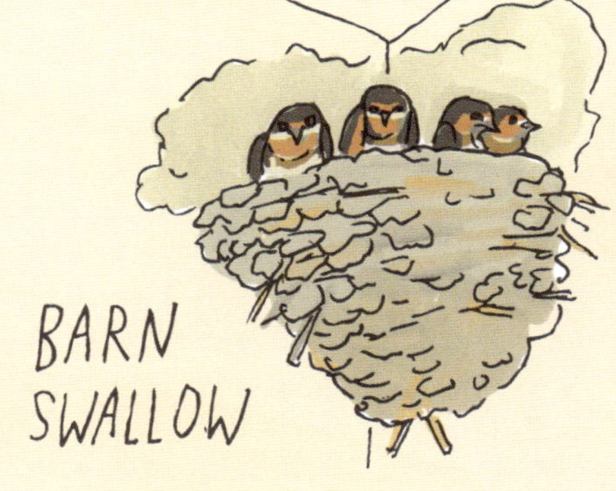

Barn Swallow

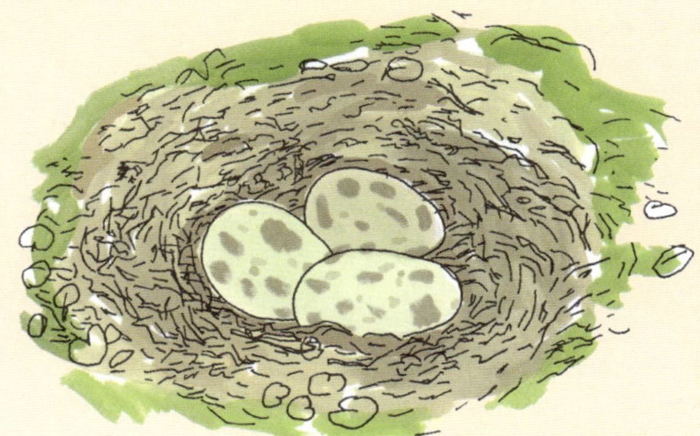

Greater Black-Backed Gull

BIRDS OF PREY

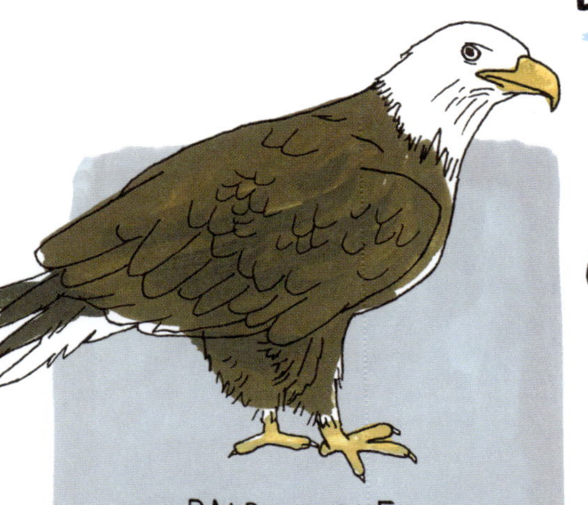

BALD EAGLE

builds massive nests made of sticks, often found near water where it hunts for fish

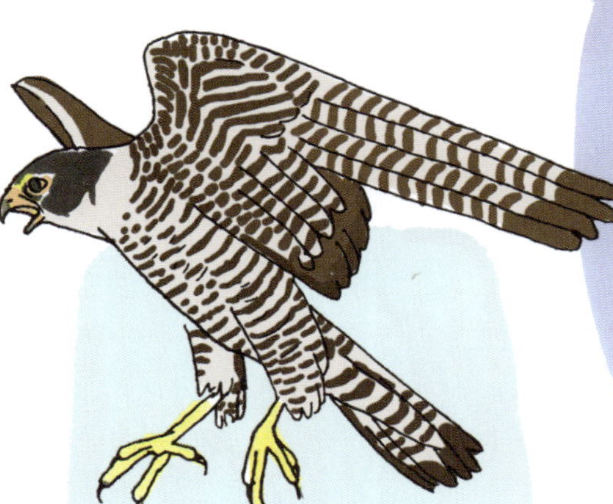

PEREGRINE FALCON

has been recorded diving at over 250 miles per hour

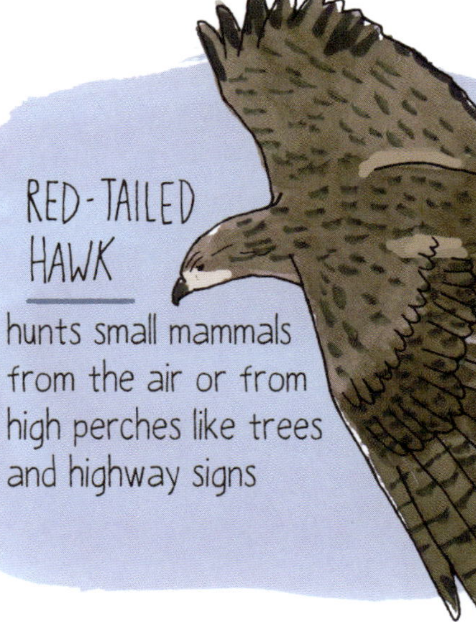

RED-TAILED HAWK

hunts small mammals from the air or from high perches like trees and highway signs

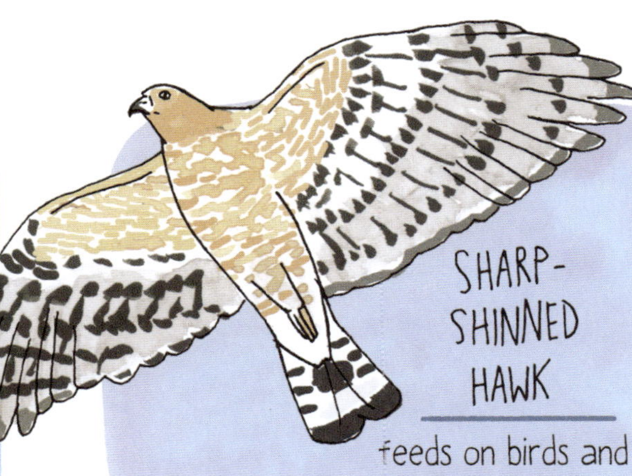

SHARP-SHINNED HAWK

feeds on birds and small mammals

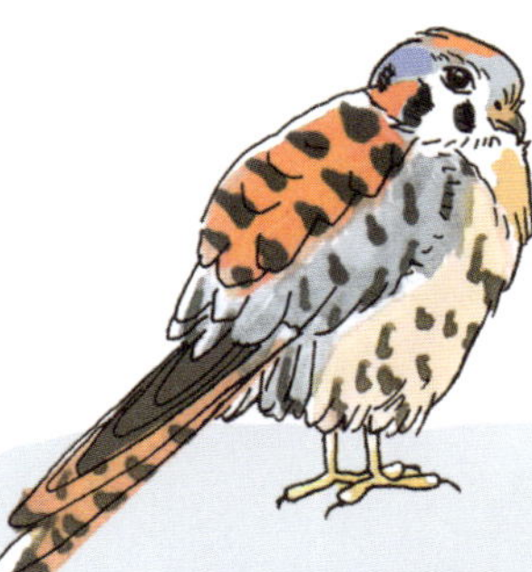

AMERICAN KESTREL

hovers above small mammals before quickly diving for the kill

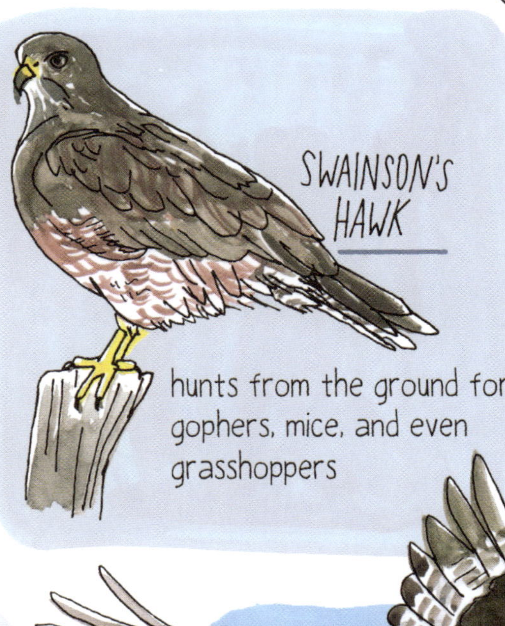

SWAINSON'S HAWK

hunts from the ground for gophers, mice, and even grasshoppers

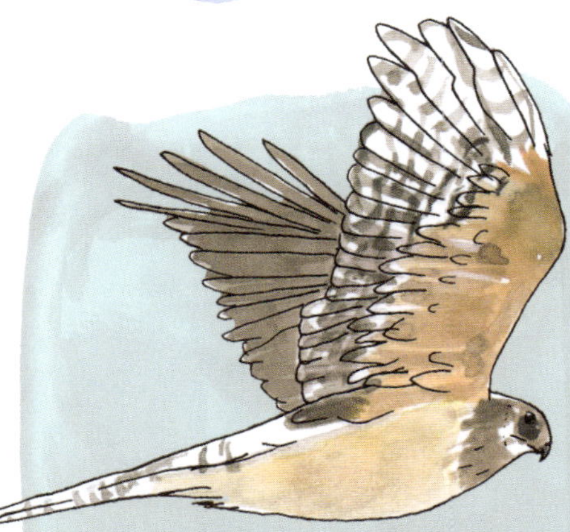

NORTHERN HARRIER

also called the marsh hawk, builds nests on the ground

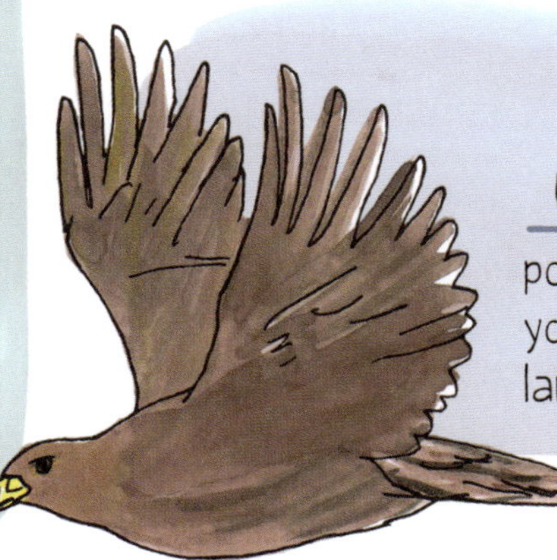

GOLDEN EAGLE

powerful enough to hunt young deer and other large mammals

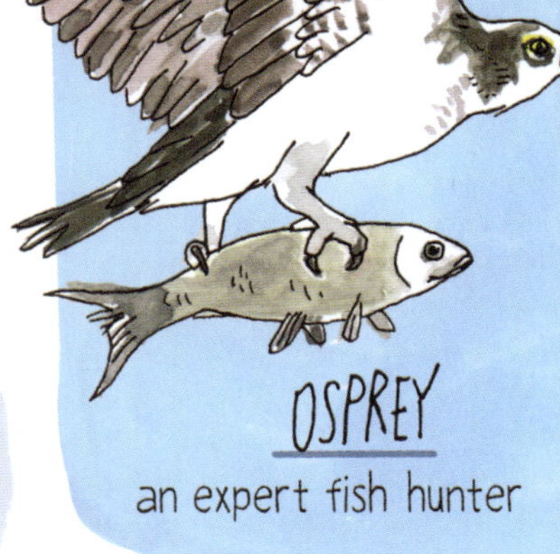

OSPREY

an expert fish hunter

WATER BODIES

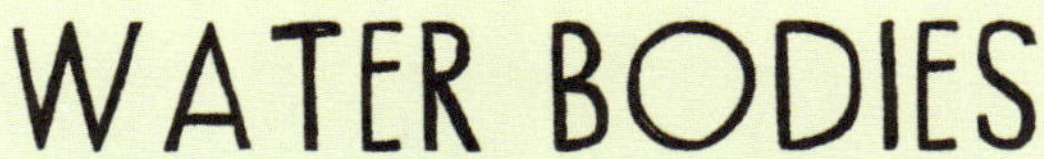

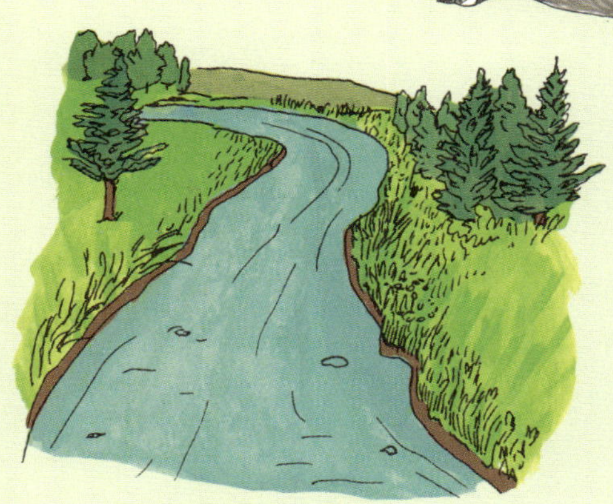

RIVER
a natural waterway that flows toward another body of water

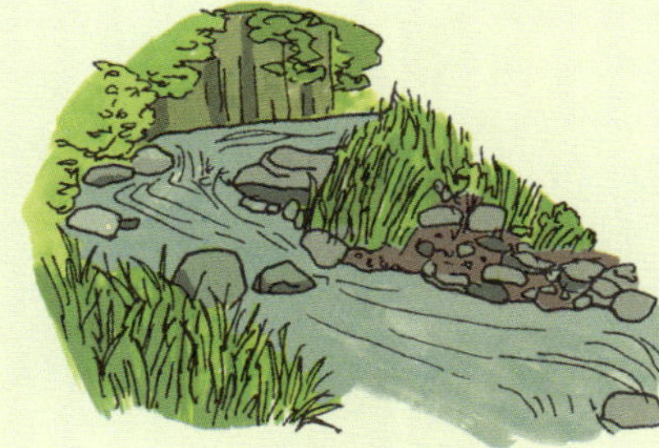

STREAM
a small to medium body of flowing water held between banks

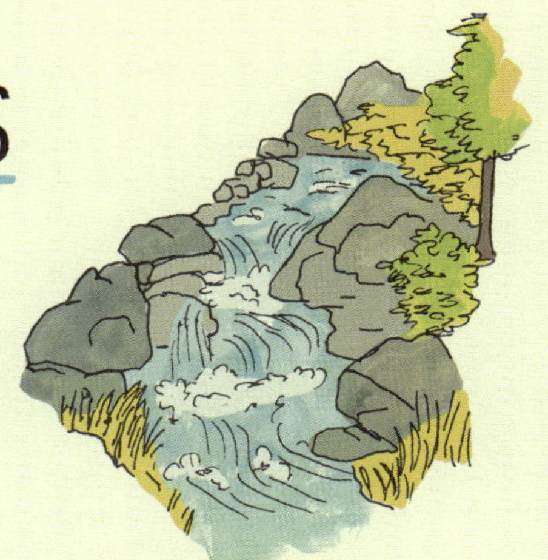

BROOK
a small stream

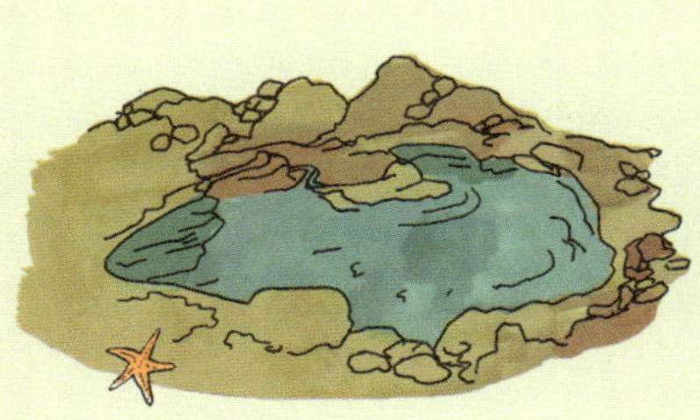

TIDAL POOL
rocky saltwater shore pools that become separate from the ocean during low tide

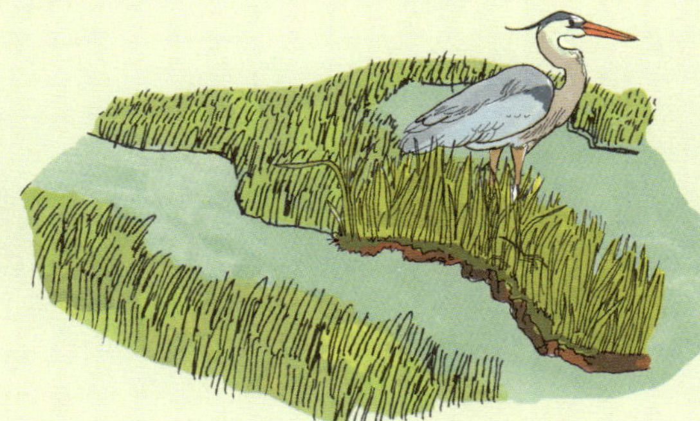

MARSH
a wetland with herbaceous plant life but no trees

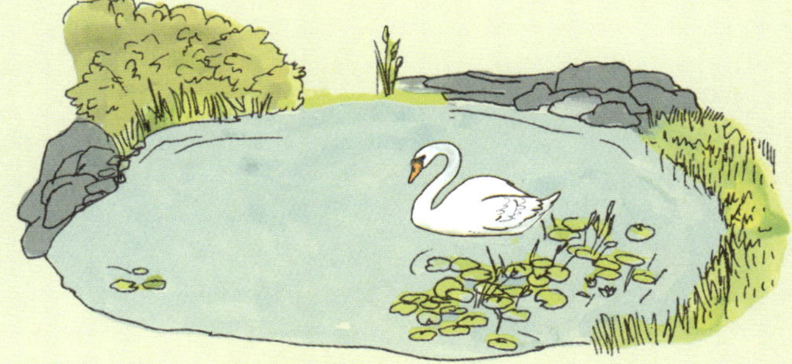

POND
a body of standing water too small for significant waves or depth-based temperature variations

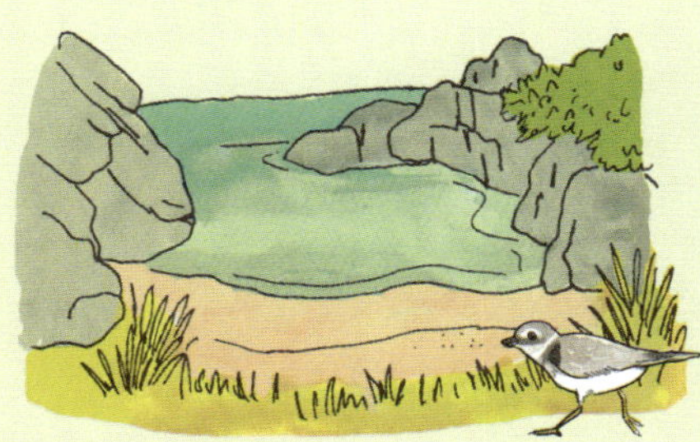

COVE a small bay

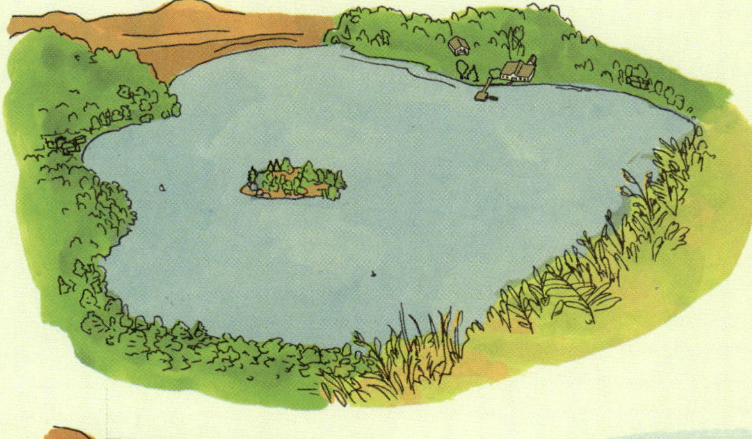

LAKE
a basin of still water larger than a pond

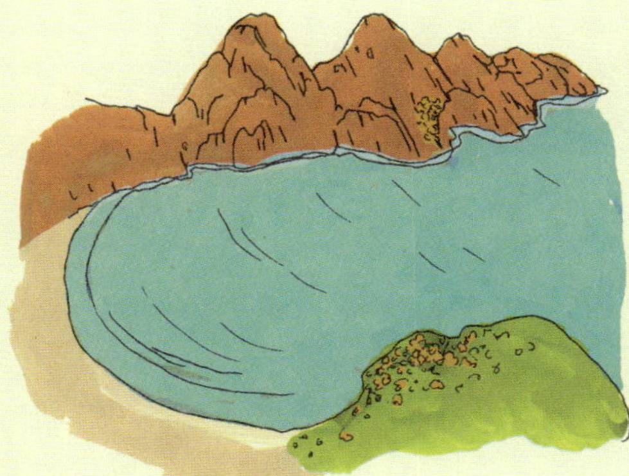

BAY
a broad inlet partially surrounded by land

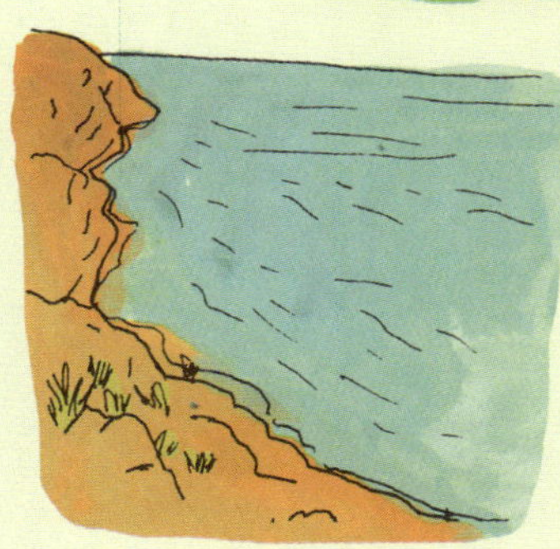

SEA
a large body of salt water that is smaller than an ocean and sometimes bordered by land

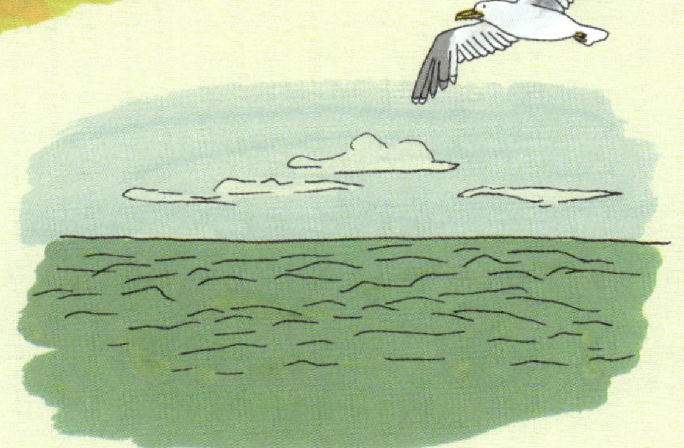

OCEAN
massive bodies of salt water that cover nearly two-thirds of the earth's surface

BUTTERFLIES

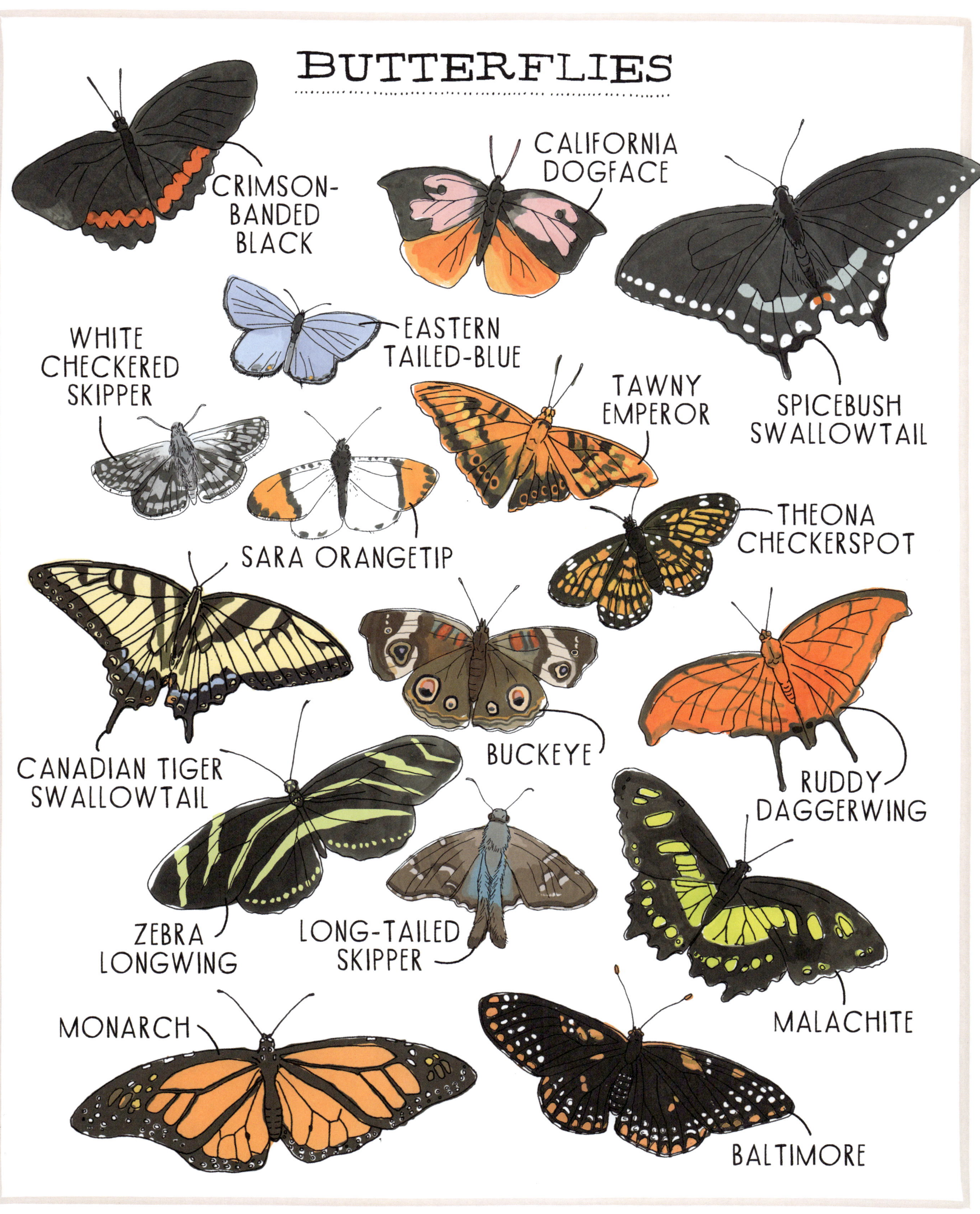

ANATOMY OF A BUTTERFLY

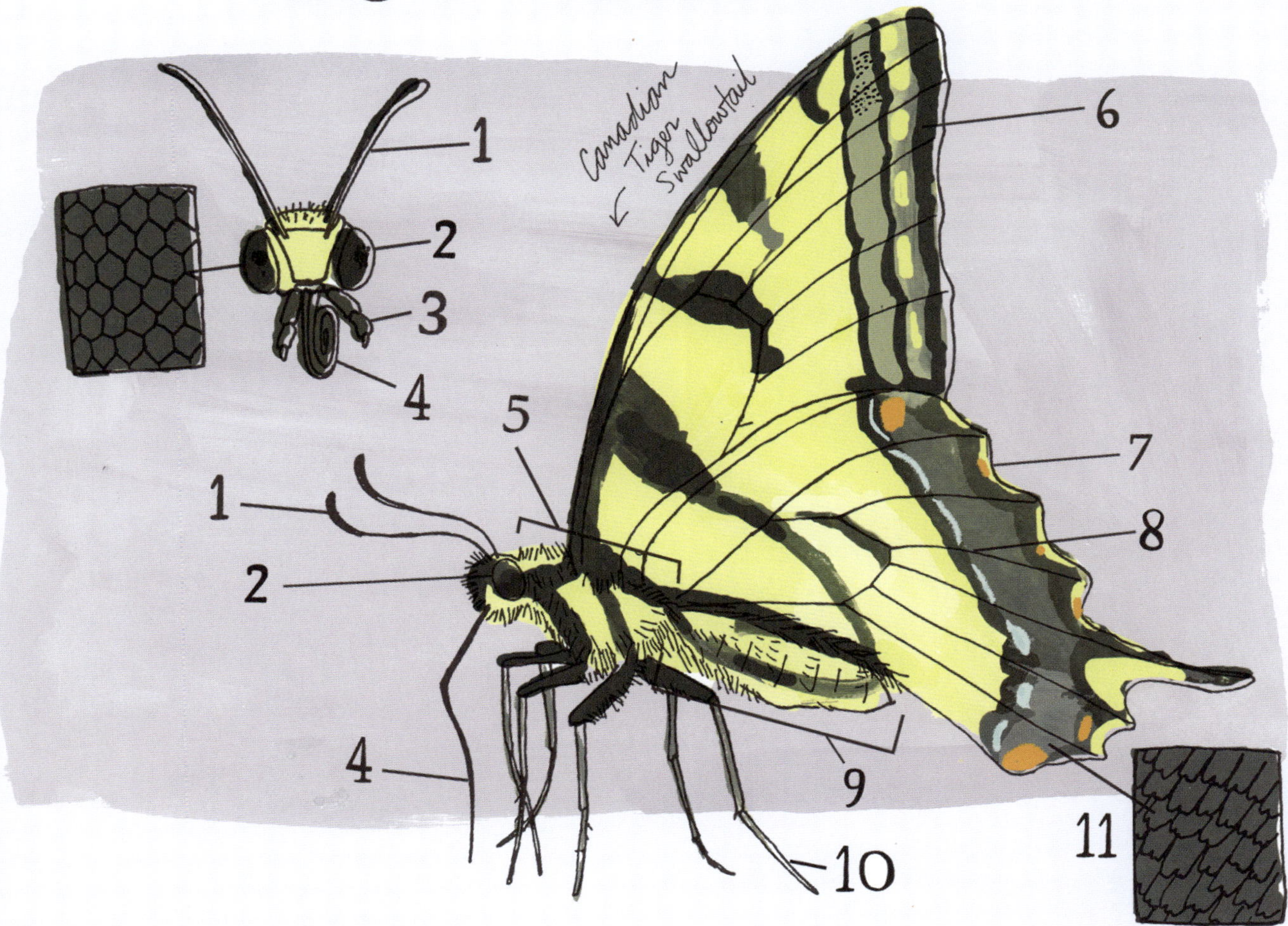

1. **antenna** - used as a form of radar and pheromone detection

2. **compound eye** - has up to 1,700 individual ommatidia (light receptors and lenses)

3. **palpus** - shields the eye from dust, covered in scent-detecting sensors

4. **proboscis** - like a long straw for feeding and drinking

5. **thorax** - three body segments that contain the flight muscles

6. **forewing**
7. **hindwing** — two pairs of overlapping wings that flap and sometimes glide

8. **wing veins** - vary between each genus of butterfly, used in classification

9. **abdomen** - contains the digestive system, respiratory equipment, heart, and sex organs

10. **legs** - butterflies have three pairs except in the Nymphalidae family

11. **scales** - wings are covered in tiny dustlike colored scales

KINDS OF CLOUDS

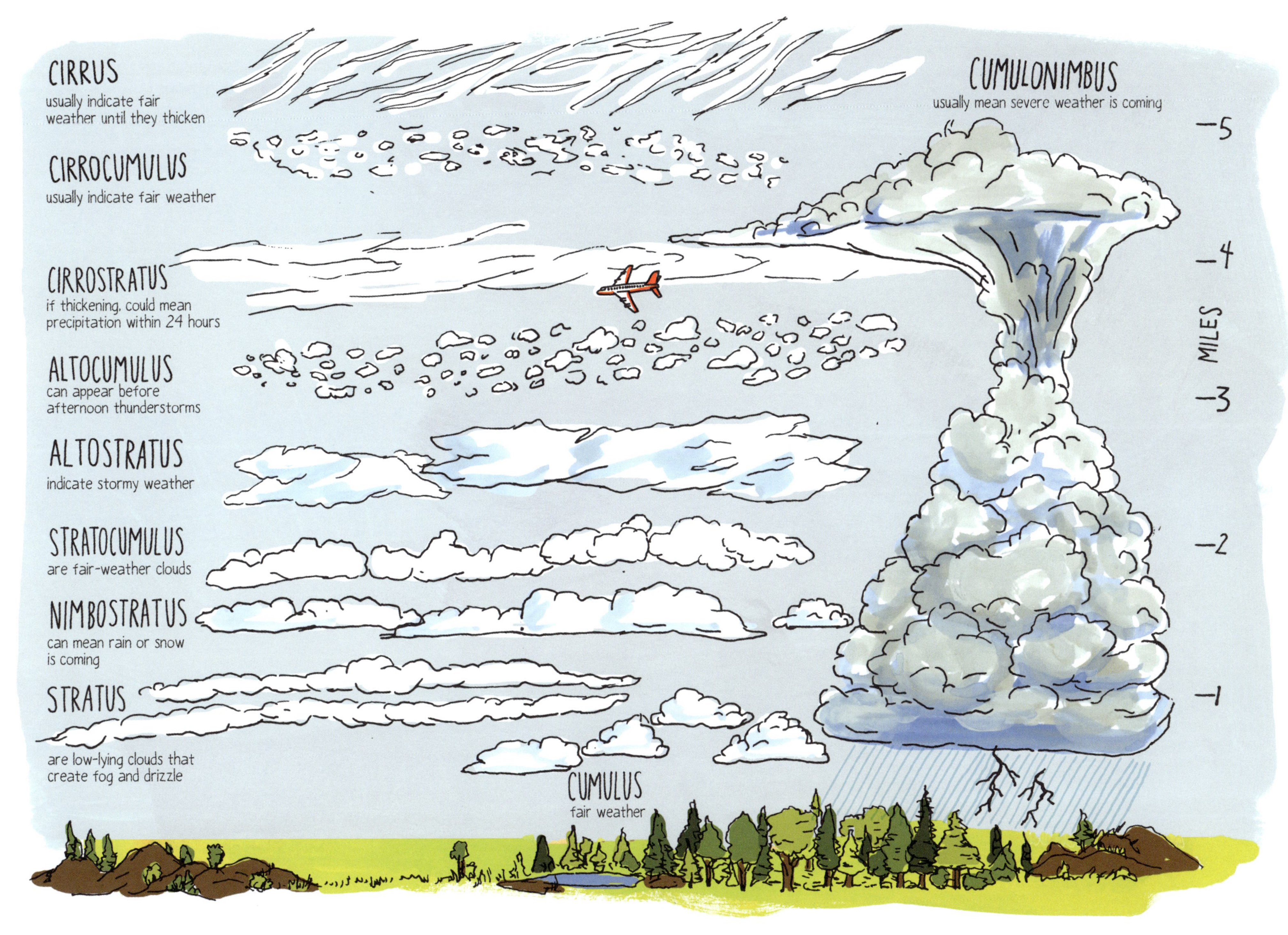

COMMON COLD-BLOODED CREATURES

(SNAKES, SALAMANDERS, LIZARDS, AND TURTLES)

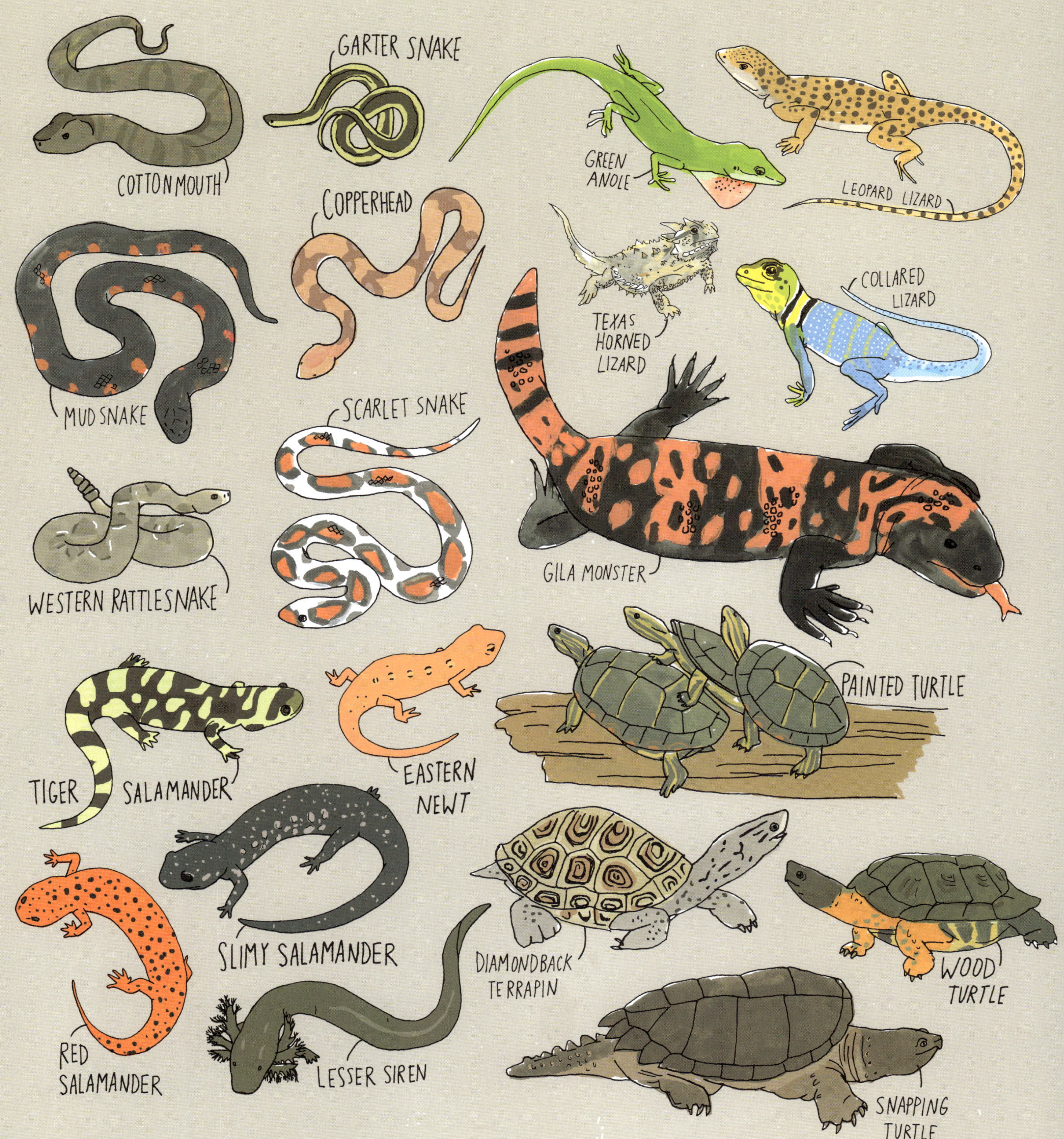

Extraordinary Eggs

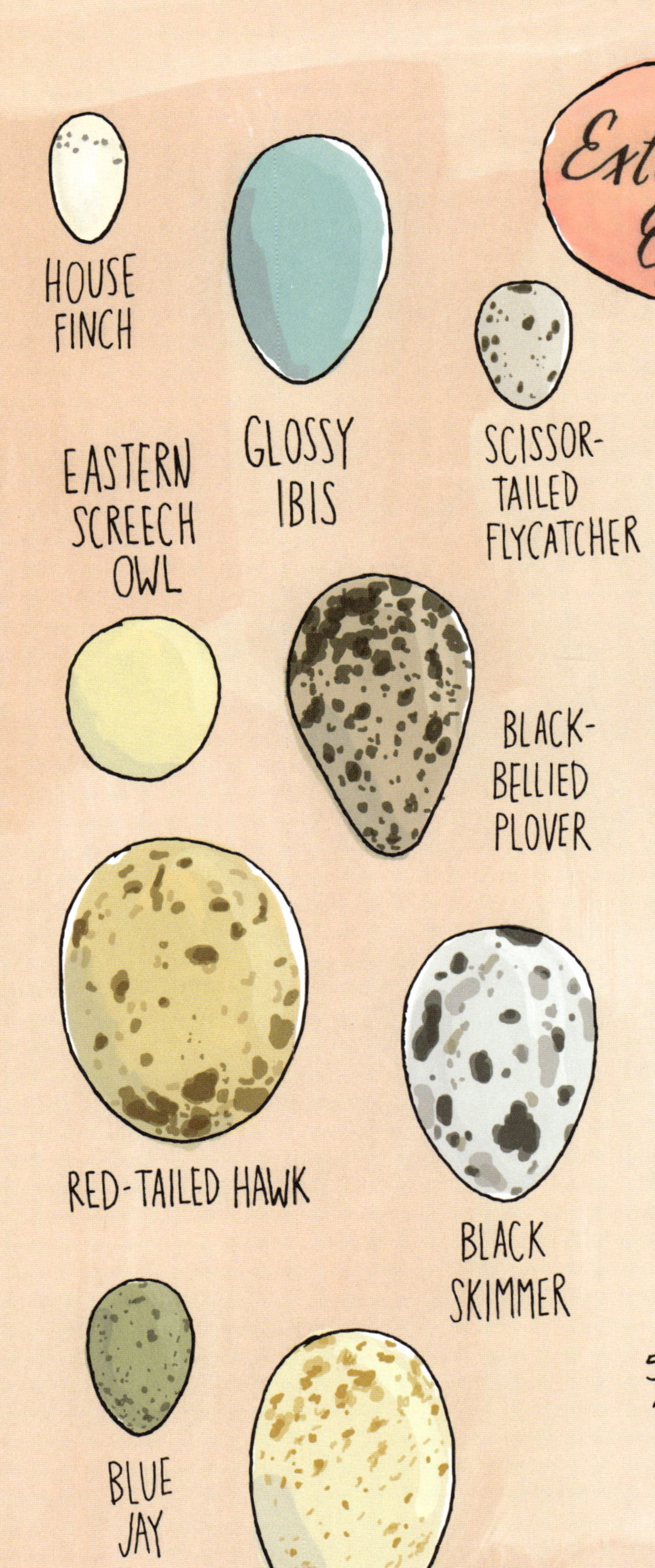

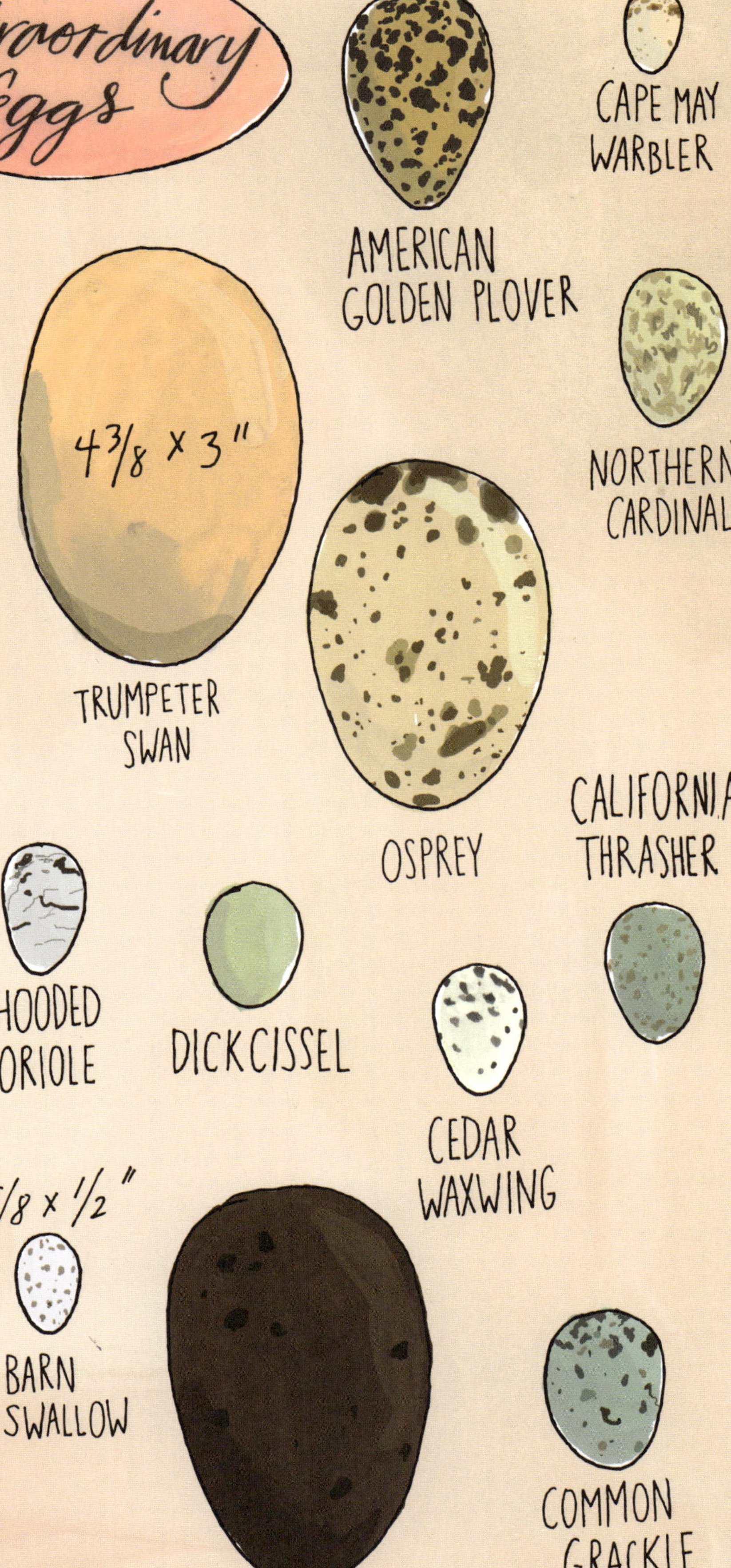

FIERCE + FURRY

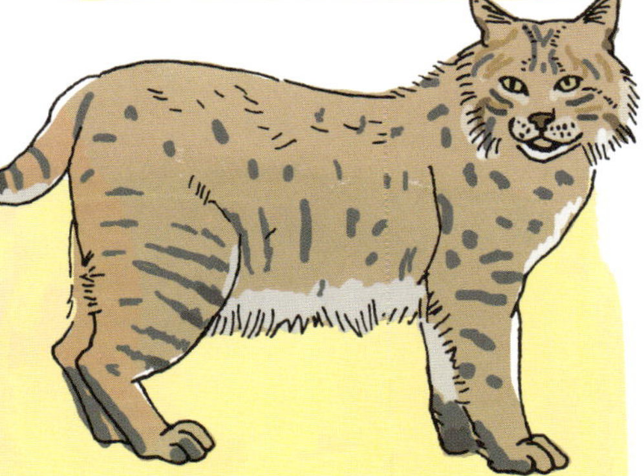

LITTLE BROWN BAT

Although it sleeps almost 20 hours per day, when it's awake, it can catch between 600 and 1,200 insects in an hour.

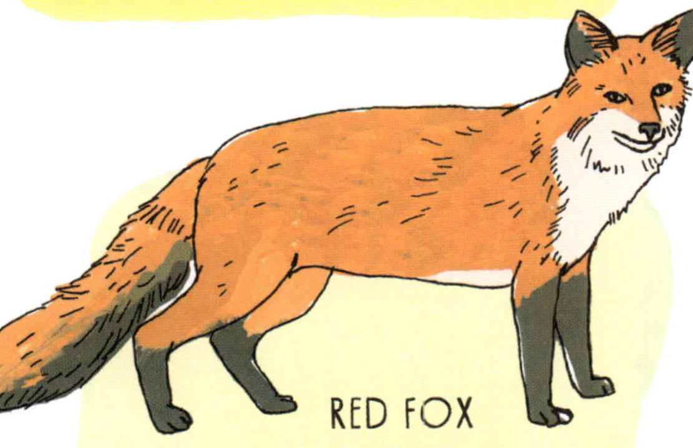

BOBCAT

Named for its stubby tail, the bobcat is smaller than its northern lynx cousin and lacks the distinctive ear tufts.

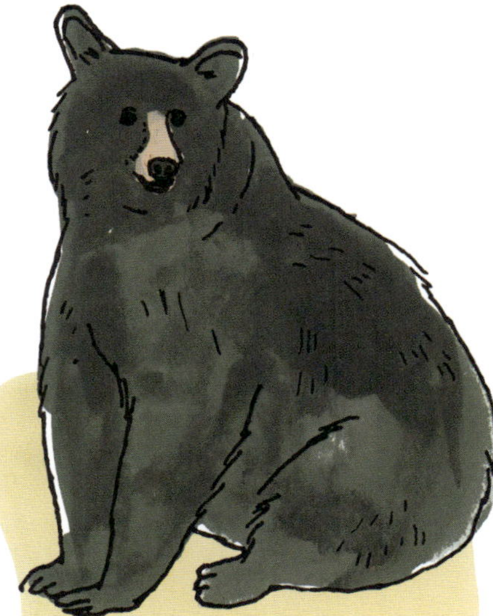

BLACK BEAR

With strong, sharp claws, black bears can climb 100 feet of a tree in about 30 seconds.

MOUNTAIN LION

More closely related to the domestic cat than the lion, the mountain lion's range extends from northern Canada to southern South America.

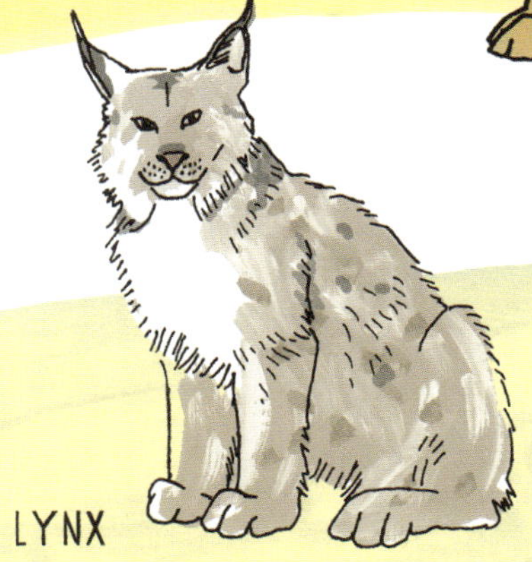

LYNX

In the snowy north, a lynx's paw may be larger than a human's hand.

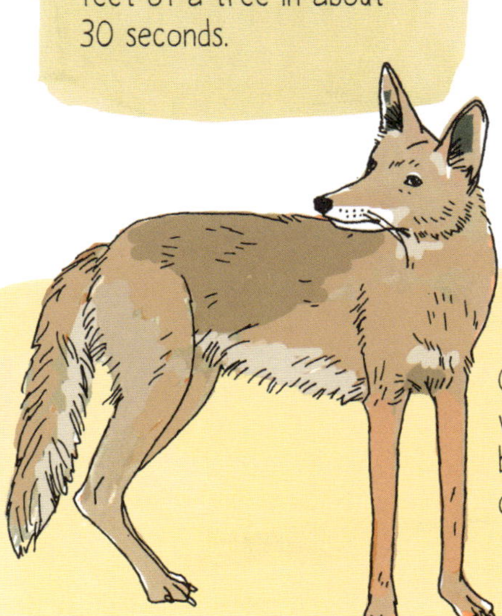

RED FOX

Foxes have whiskers on their legs as well as their faces, to help them find their way.

COYOTE

Coyotes communicate with a wide variety of sounds: howls, barks, growls, high-pitched crying, wails, and even squeals.

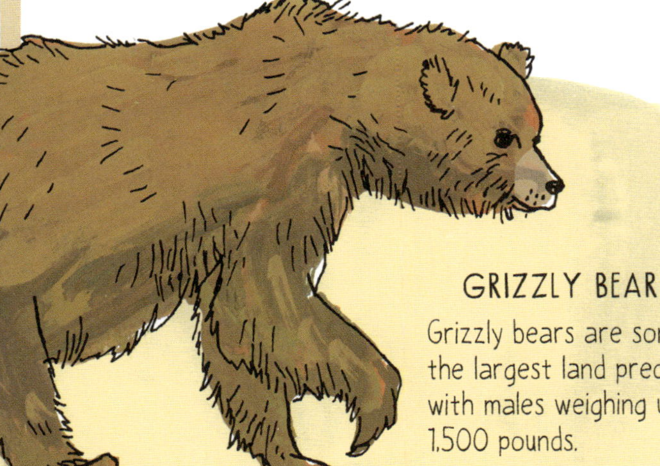

GRIZZLY BEAR

Grizzly bears are some of the largest land predators with males weighing up to 1,500 pounds.

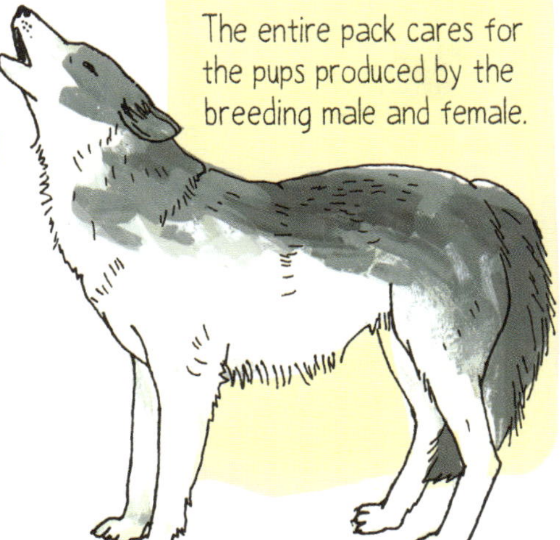

GRAY WOLF

The entire pack cares for the pups produced by the breeding male and female.

WOLVERINE

The largest member of the weasel family, the wolverine is strong enough to take down animals much larger than itself.

ANATOMY OF A FLOWER

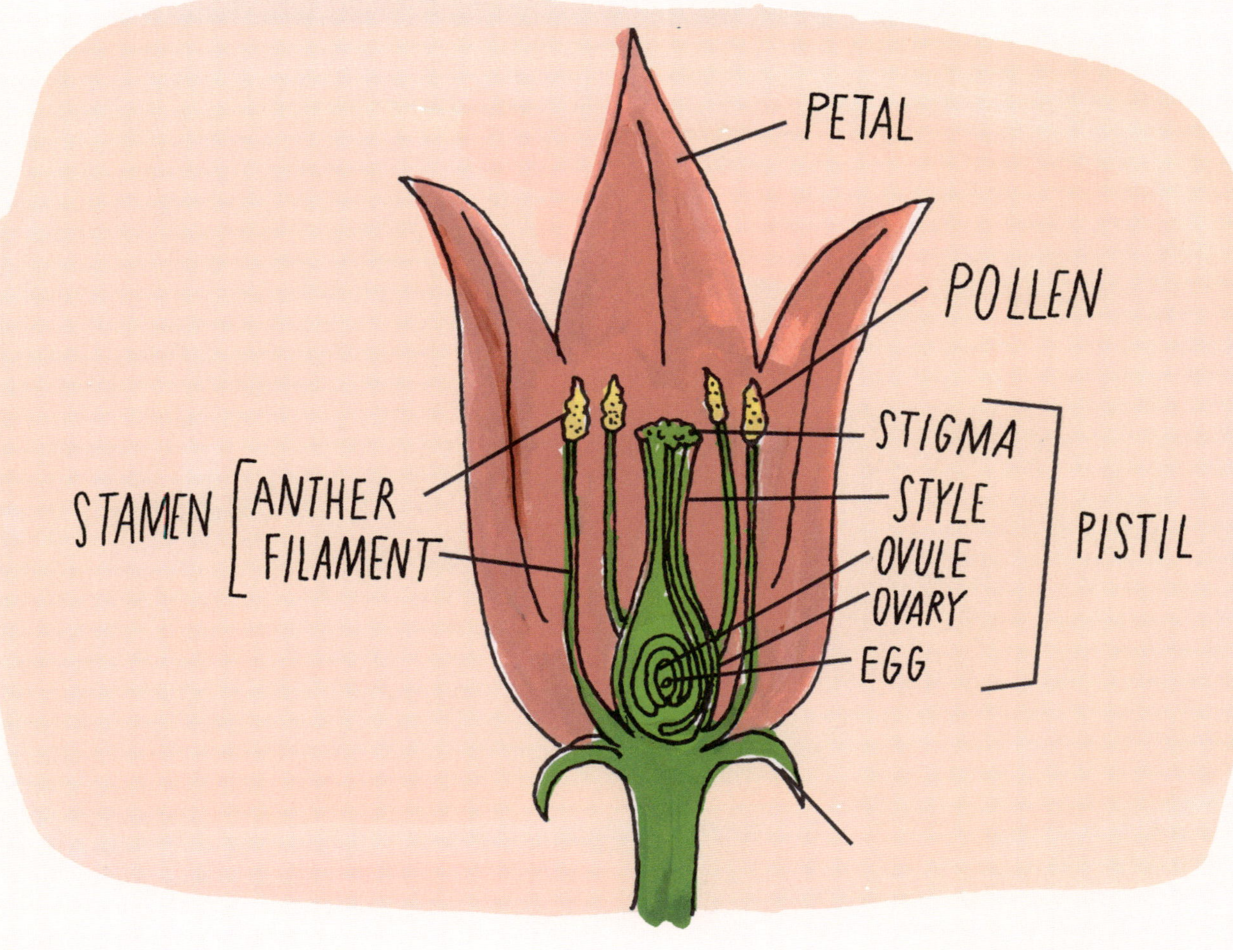

anther - male reproductive cell that contains pollen

filament - supports the anther

sepal - modified leaf beneath the flower

stamen - includes the male parts of the flower

pistil - includes the female parts of the flower

ovary - female reproductive organ

ovule - reproductive cell; forms the seed when fertilized with pollen

stigma - structure atop the ovary that receives pollen

style - stalk that connects the stigma and the ovary

FLOWERS, CONES, SEEDS + FRUITS OF TREES

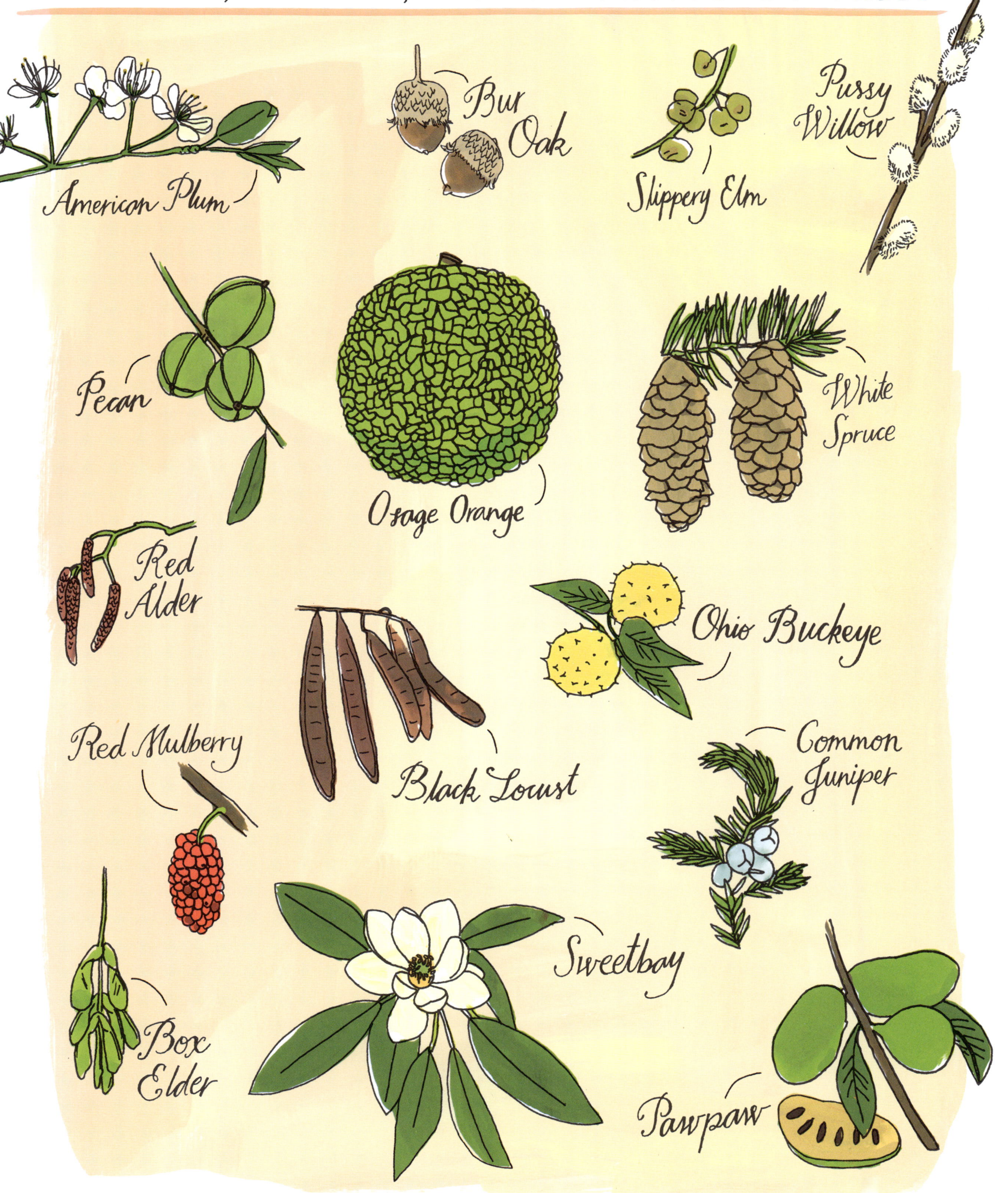

INSECTS AND SPIDERS

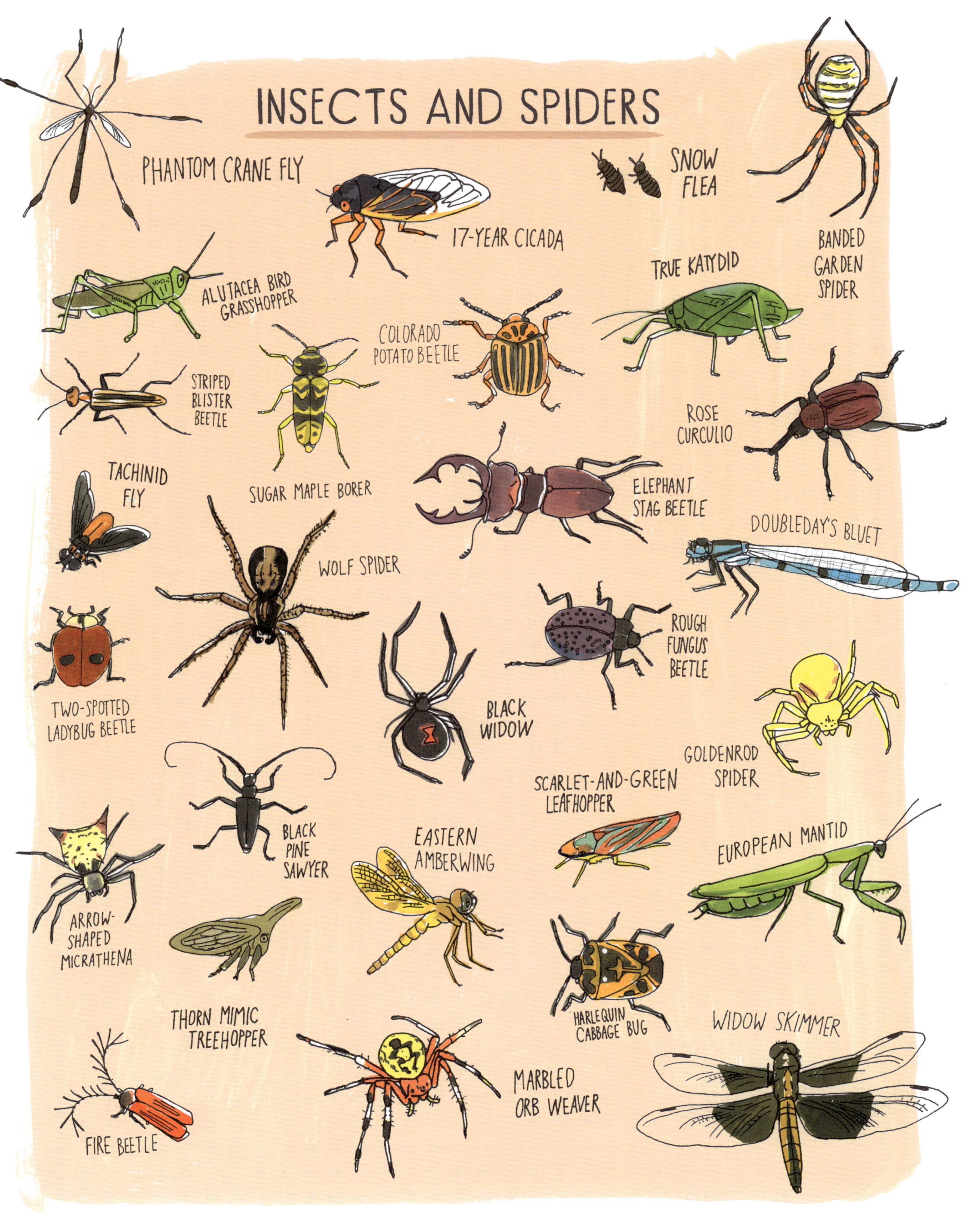

LANDFORMS

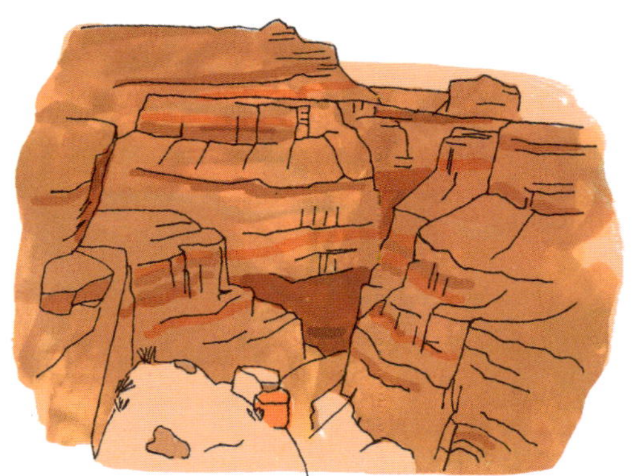

CANYON

a deep river valley with very steep sides, carved into the land by rivers over long periods of time

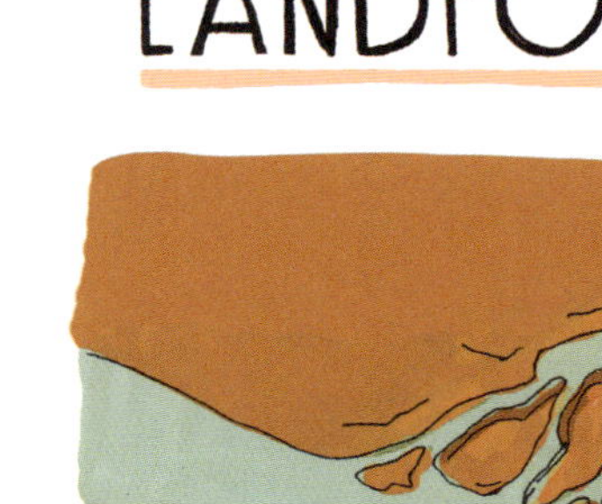

DELTA

a low, triangular formation at the mouth of a river where silt, sand, and small rocks are deposited where the river meets a larger body of water

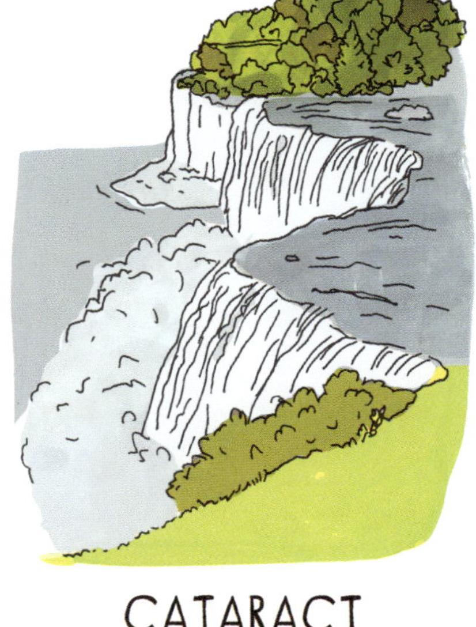

CATARACT

a large and powerful waterfall

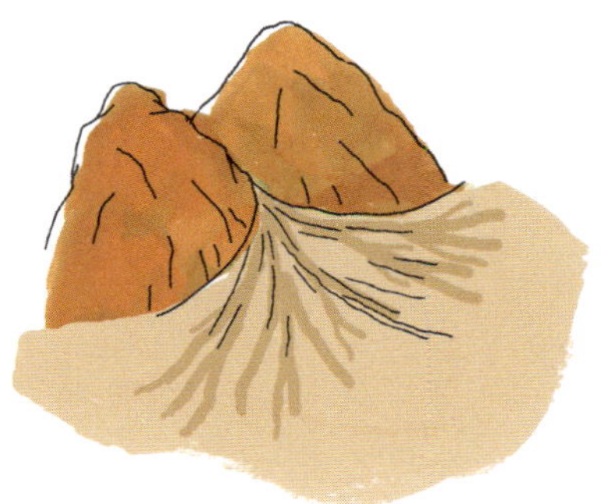

ALLUVIAL FAN

made of large amounts of sediment deposited by streams and rivers in a fan shape

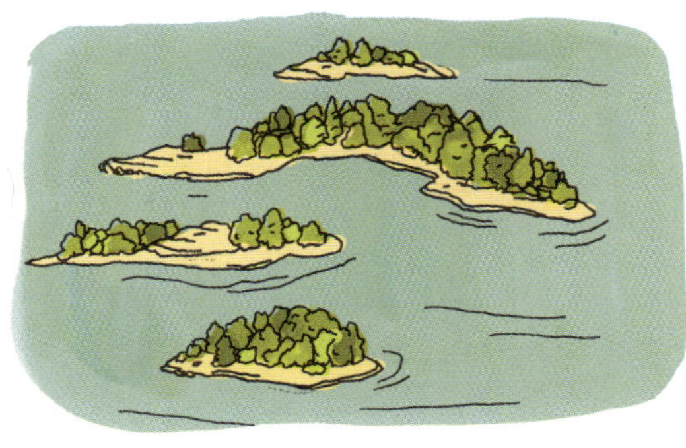

ARCHIPELAGO

a cluster or chain of islands found in a sea or ocean

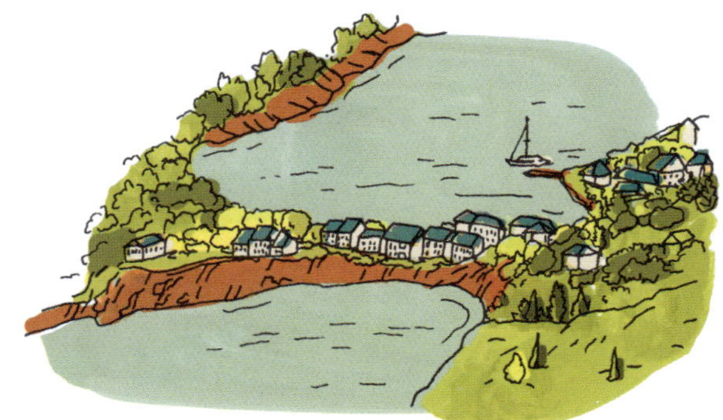

ISTHMUS

a narrow bridge of land connecting two larger land masses across a body of water

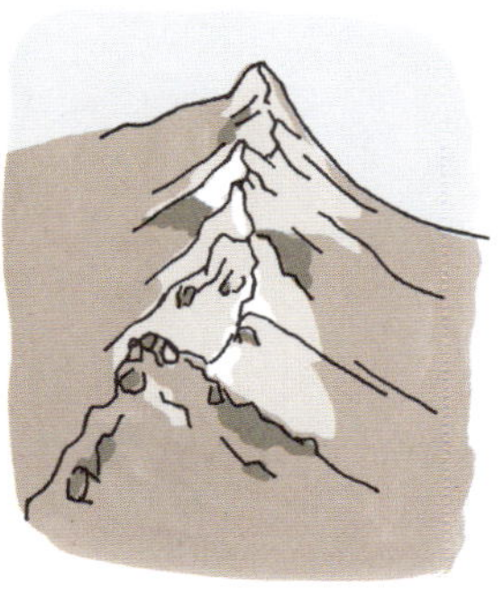

ARÊTE

a thin ridge of rock left between the erosion paths of two parallel glaciers

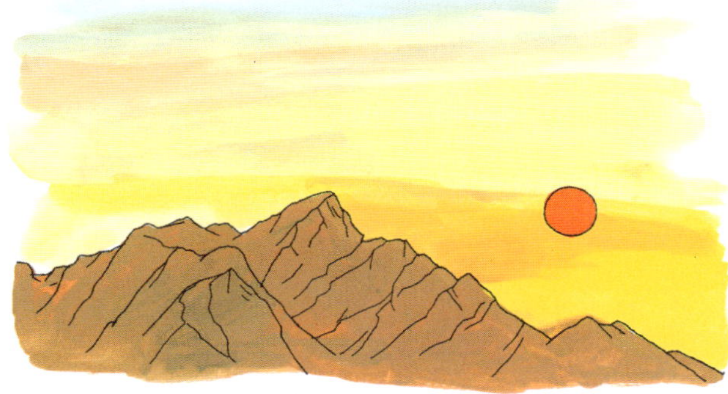

MOUNTAIN

formed over long periods of time by plate tectonics, the process by which large pieces of the earth's crust shift, collide, crumple, and slide

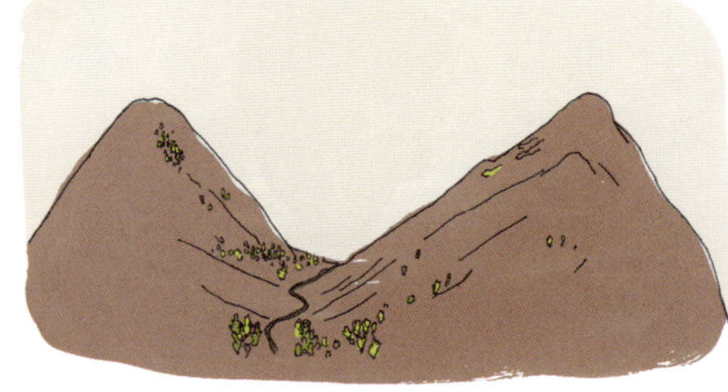

COL

the lowest point on a mountain ridge between two peaks, also called a gap, notch, or saddle

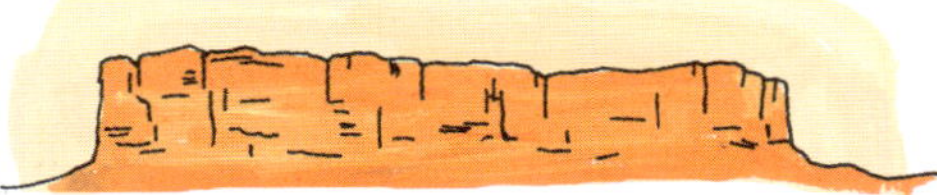

PLATEAU

a massive area of flat terrain that is higher than the surrounding area

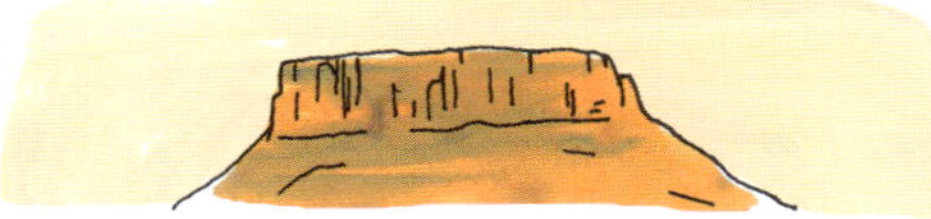

MESA

a smaller area of elevated arid land with a flat top and sides that are usually steep cliffs

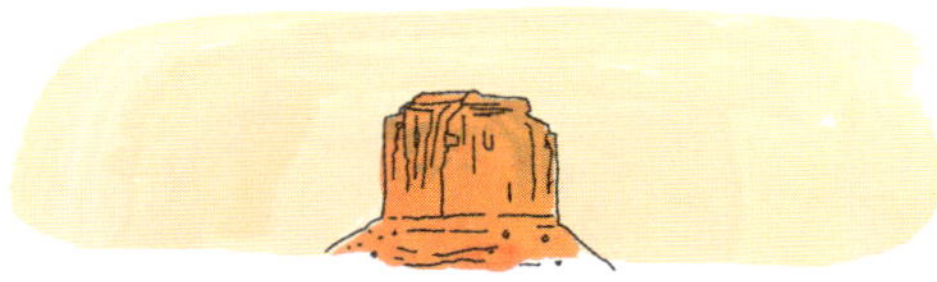

BUTTE

an even smaller area of raised land with steep sides. Most buttes were once larger mesas.

MARINE MAMMALS

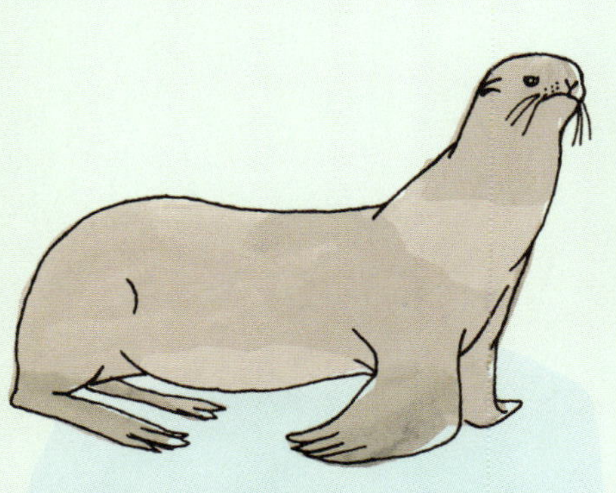

NORTHERN FUR SEAL

Dense, luxurious fur keeps these seals insulated in the cold north. Males fight for breeding grounds, and once they've won a space they stay put, fasting through the entire breeding season.

NORTHERN ELEPHANT SEAL

Excellent deep-sea divers, they can remain underwater for up to 2 hours. Males grow to 20 feet long and are fiercely protective of their harems. They roar and bellow through their long noses during the mating season.

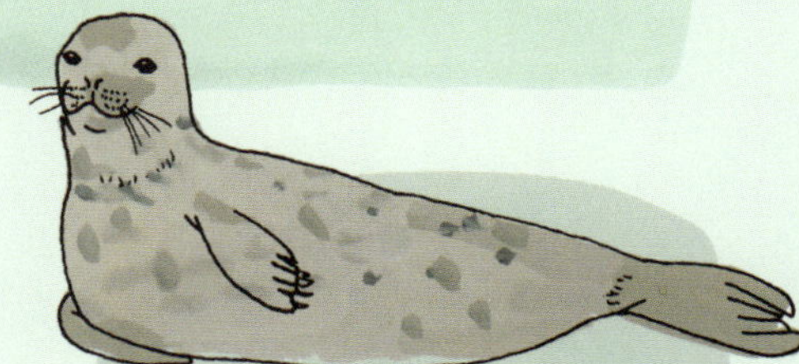

MANATEE

Fond of the warm water flowing out of power plants, these slow-moving mammals graze on sea-bottom plants with their nimble, prehensile lips.

CALIFORNIA SEA LION

These playful swimmers can be seen leaping from the water and riding waves like surfers. They feed at night on fish and mollusks.

HARBOR SEAL

These seals spend a lot of time on shore and are comfortable mating on land or at sea. They've been known to give birth in the water.

BOTTLENOSE DOLPHIN

These social creatures use echolocation to hunt. They communicate with body language and clicks and squeaks from their mouths and blowholes.

ORCA

Master pack hunters, orcas corral fish into tight coves where they are easy to catch. They can hunt a whale many times their size by chasing one down and taking bites until the whale succumbs.

HUMPBACK WHALE

These whales migrate 15,000 miles per year between polar feeding areas and warm-water mating grounds.

HARBOR PORPOISE

Elaborate courtship displays between males and females may involve intense vocalizations and playful touching.

SEA OTTER

The smallest marine mammal spends almost all of its time in the water. To crack mollusks open, an otter floats on its back and smashes shells against rocks it holds on its belly.

MARVELOUS MUSHROOMS

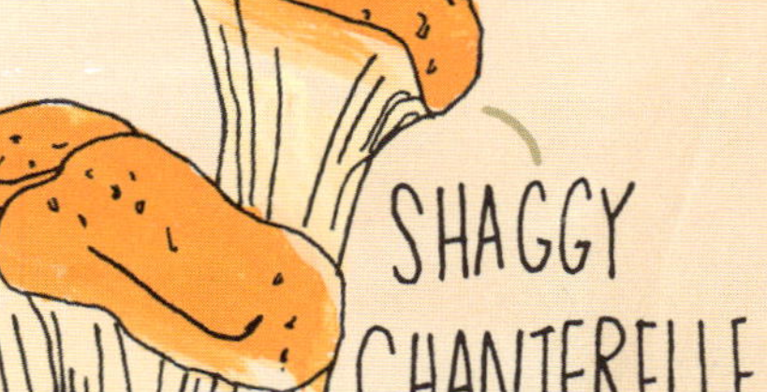

SHAGGY CHANTERELLE

This one can be toxic.

HONEY MUSHROOMS

These grow in clusters on decaying wood. Its mycelia are bioluminescent (that is, they glow in the dark) and can be harmful to living trees.

HEN OF THE WOODS

This tasty species grows in clumps at the base of oaks. Also called maitake.

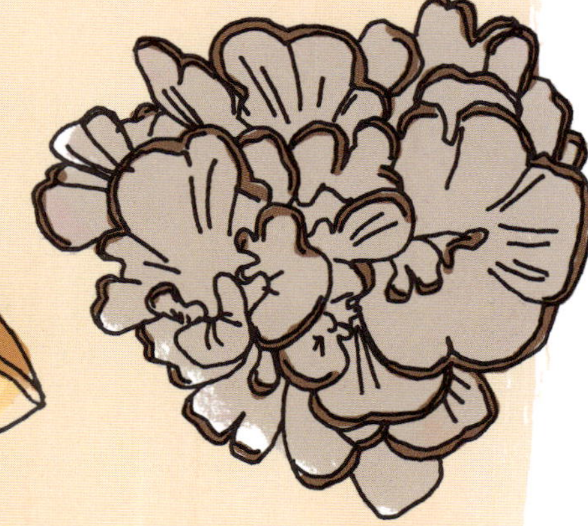

WITCH'S BUTTER

Edible but not very appealing, it can appear greasy and slimy and is sometimes called "yellow brain."

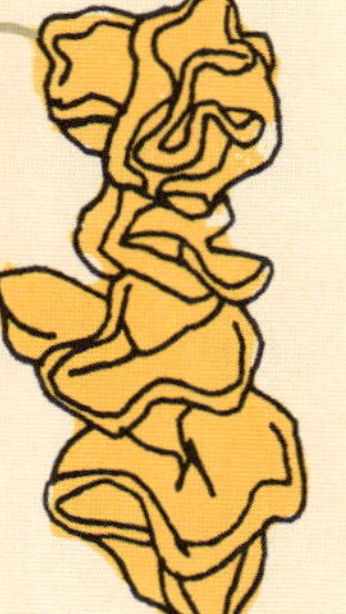

SLIPPERY JACK

Instead of gills, these mushrooms have spore-dispersing tubes on their undersides.

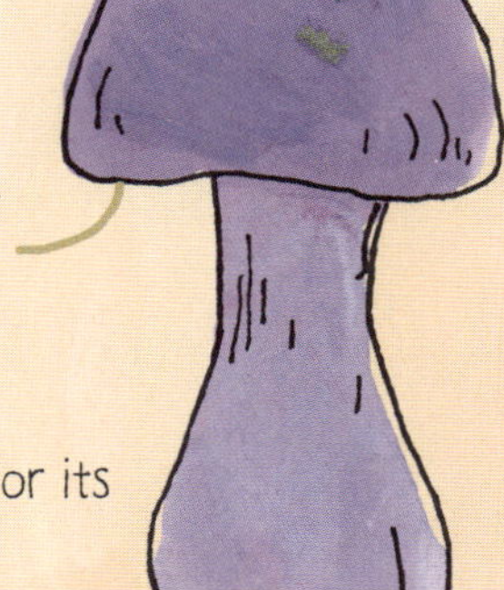

VIOLET CORT

Edible, but not choice, this one is more admired for its beautiful color.

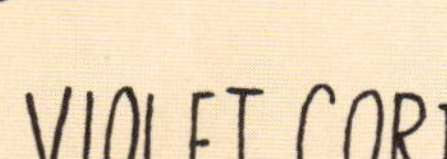

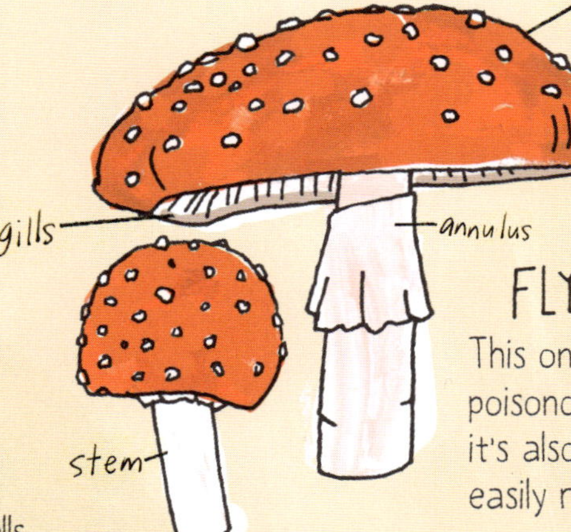

FLY AGARIC

This one is fatally poisonous if eaten; luckily, it's also one of the most easily recognizable fungi.

RAVENEL'S STINKHORN

It emits a slime that smells of rotting meat to attract flies and beetles for spore dispersal.

OYSTER MUSHROOM

This choice edible mushroom grows in clusters, attached to trees like ears.

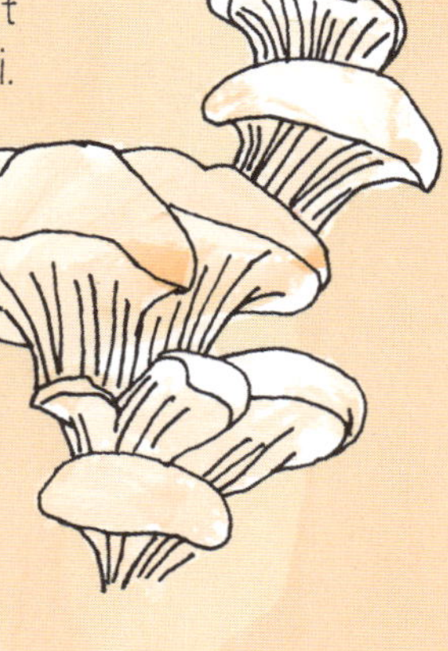

INKY CAP

It releases a liquid that can be used as ink. Edible but causes acute sensitivity to alcohol.

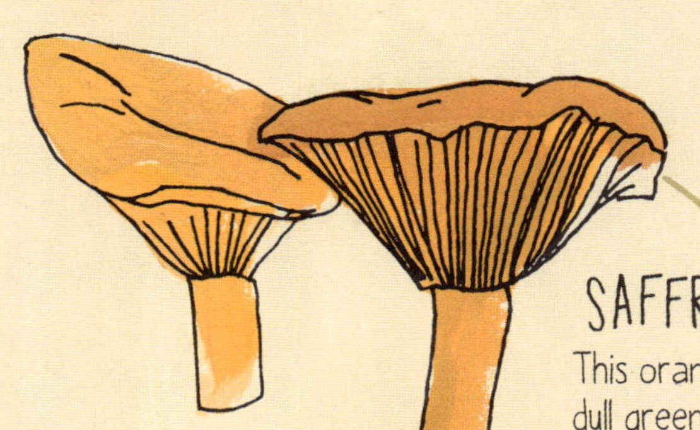

SAFFRON MILK CAP

This orange edible becomes a dull green when bruised or old.

PHASES OF THE MOON

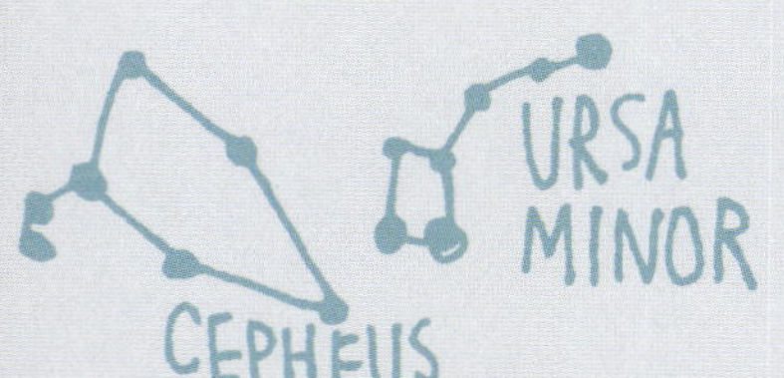

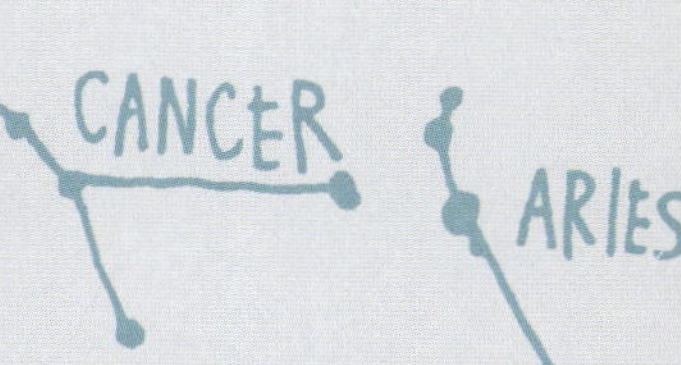

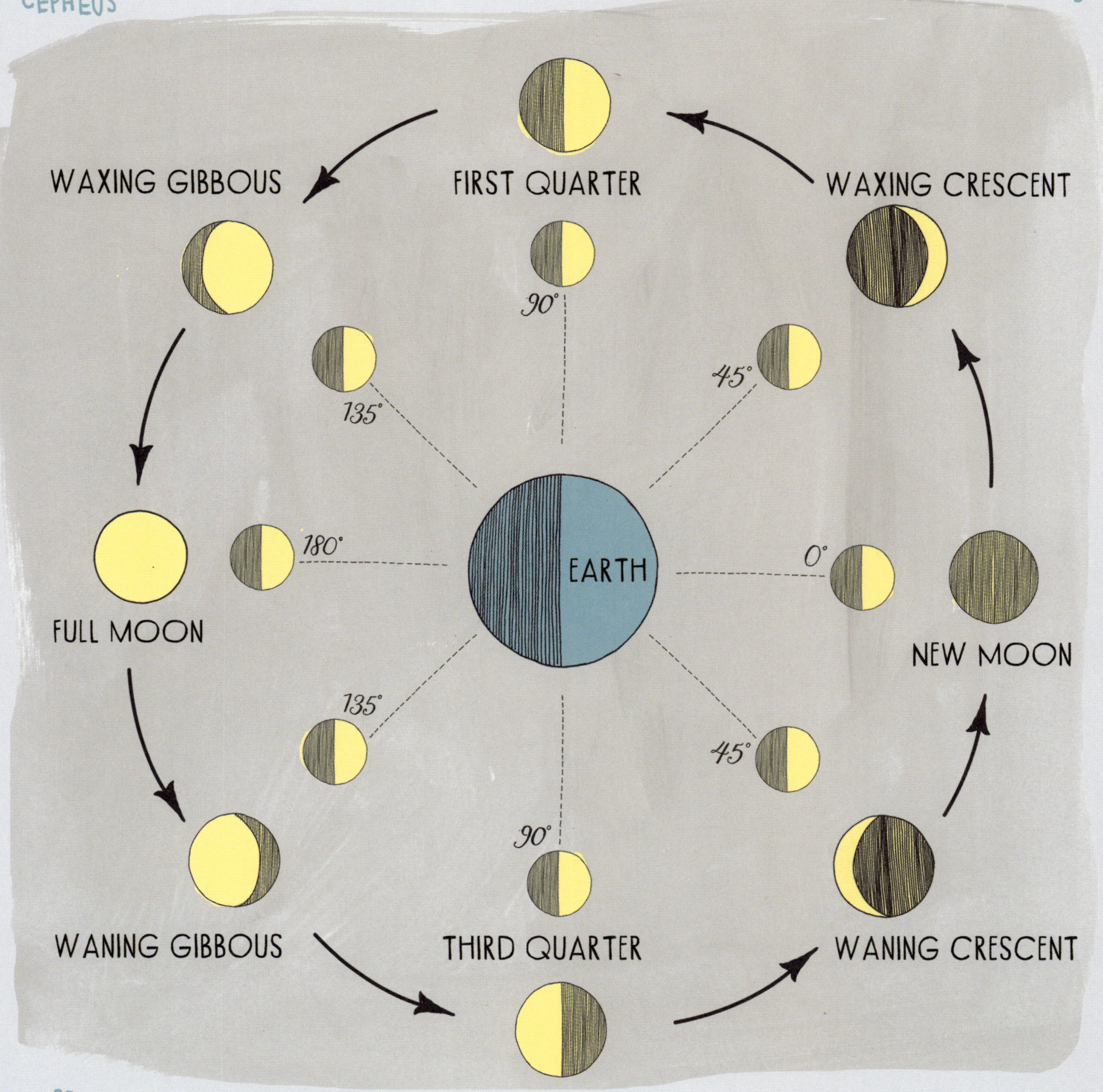

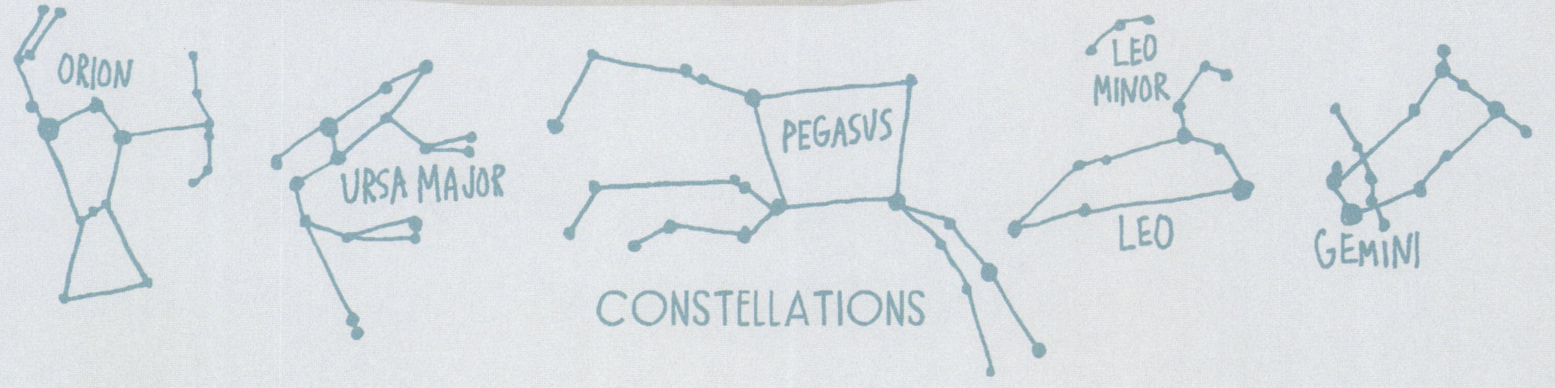

FANTASTIC SALTWATER FISH

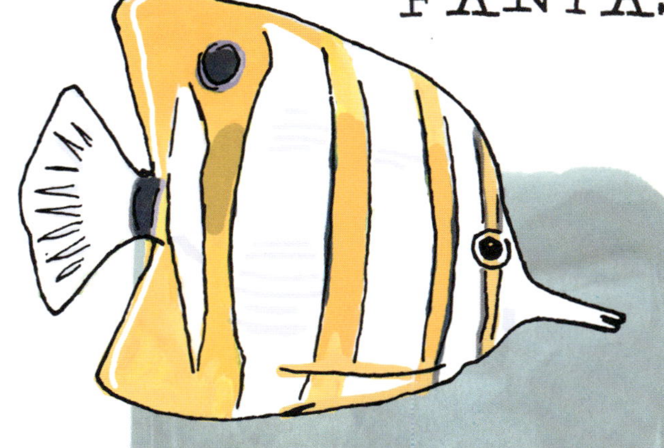

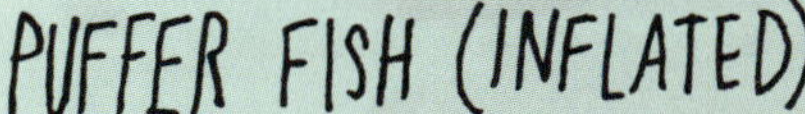

COPPERBAND BUTTERFLYFISH

The dark eye-spot on the dorsal fin confuses predators, who can't tell which way the fish will swim.

PUFFER FISH (INFLATED)

They ingest water to make themselves into a big spiny ball to ward off predators.

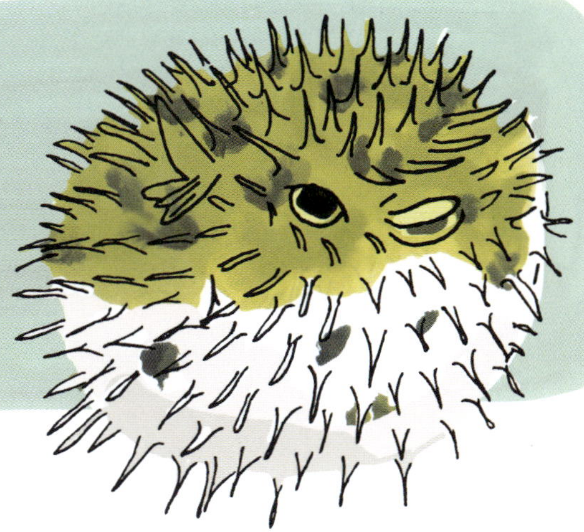

PIPEFISH

Relatives to the seahorse, these are long, slow-moving fish and usually only use their dorsal fin to swim.

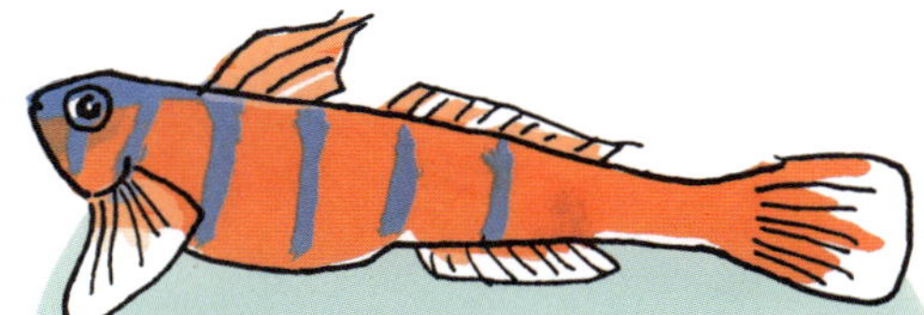

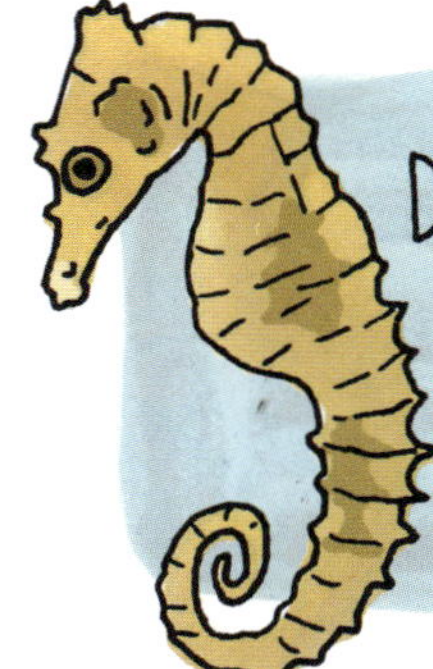

BLUEBANDED GOBY

These fish are able to change sex depending on the need within their school.

DWARF SEAHORSE

These are the slowest moving fish (about five feet per hour). Males carry the developing offspring in a pouch through gestation.

PARROTFISH

This colorful fish has a beaklike mouth to scrape up the algae and coral that form part of its diet.

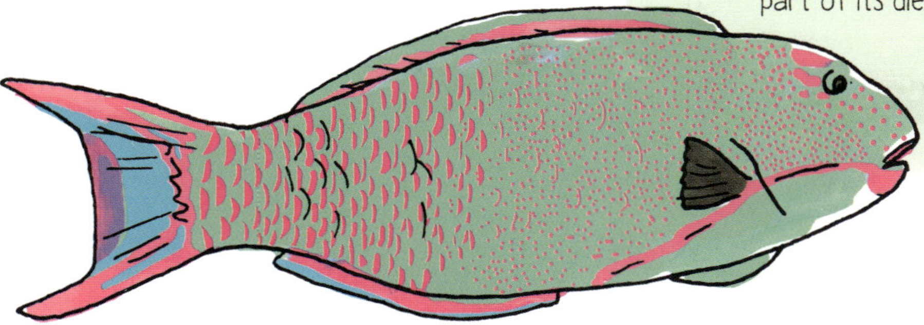

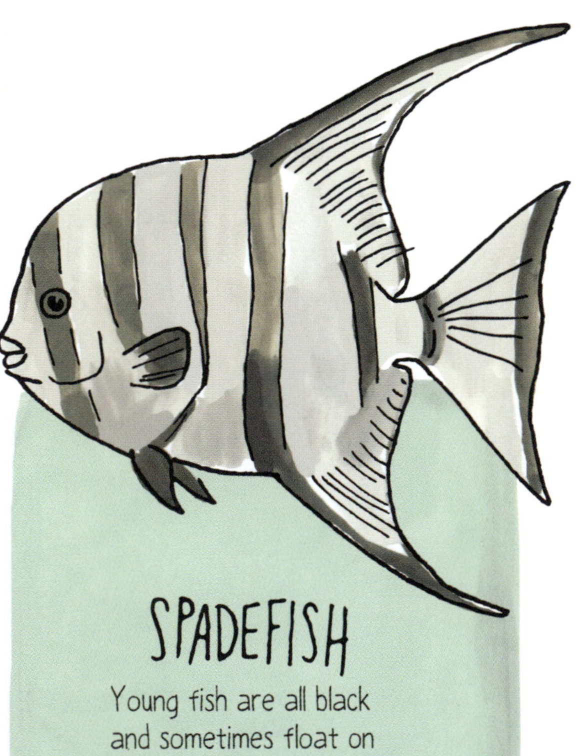

GOATFISH

These fish can change color depending on what they are doing: feeding, congregating with other fish, or resting, for example.

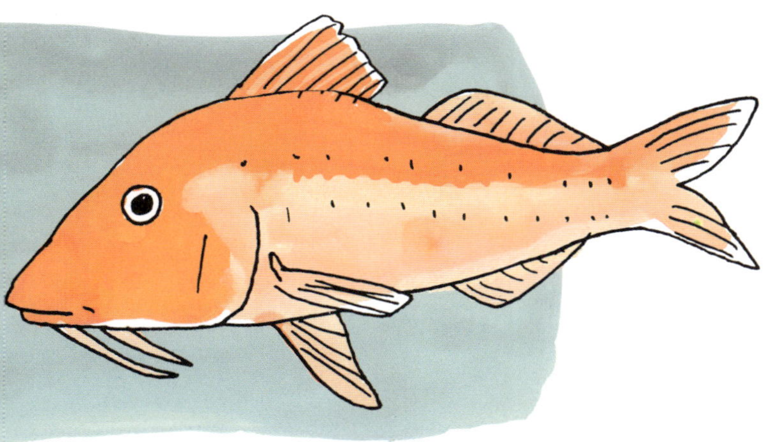

SPADEFISH

Young fish are all black and sometimes float on their sides to disguise themselves as debris.

DUNGENESS CRAB

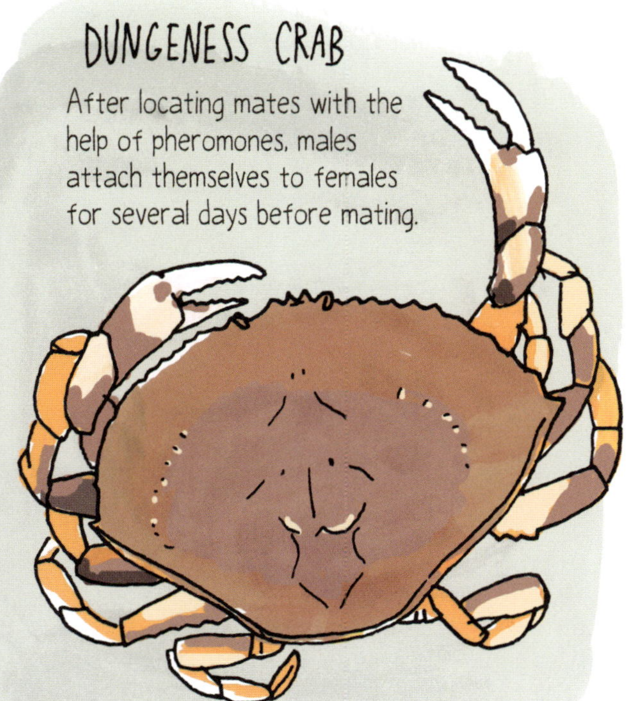

After locating mates with the help of pheromones, males attach themselves to females for several days before mating.

ON THE SAND

GEODUCK

The largest burrowing clam in the world can be longer than three feet and weigh more than two pounds. It can live hundreds of years.

MUSSELS

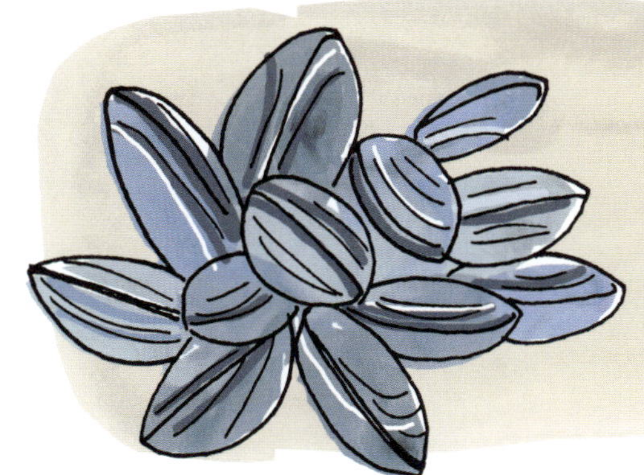

They attach themselves to underwater rocks with strong byssal threads. These gluey threads are being researched for surgical and industrial applications.

SKATE EGG CASE

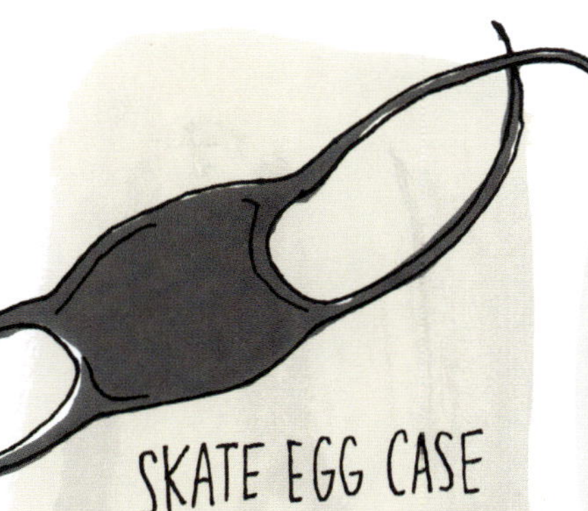

These often wash up on the shore after the fish has hatched out.

OYSTER

Of the many different species of oysters, only a few produce commercial-grade pearls.

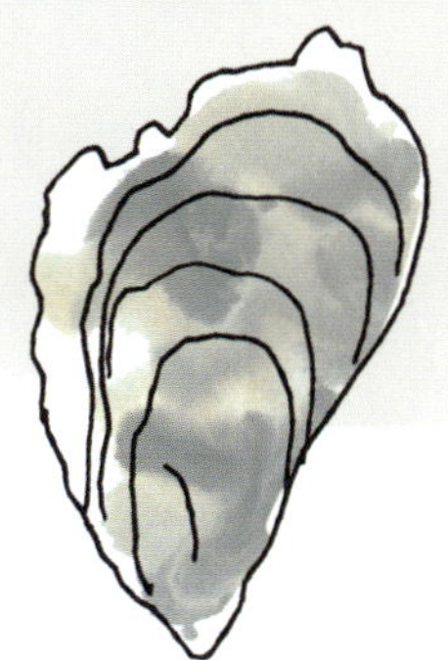

ATLANTIC BLUE CRAB

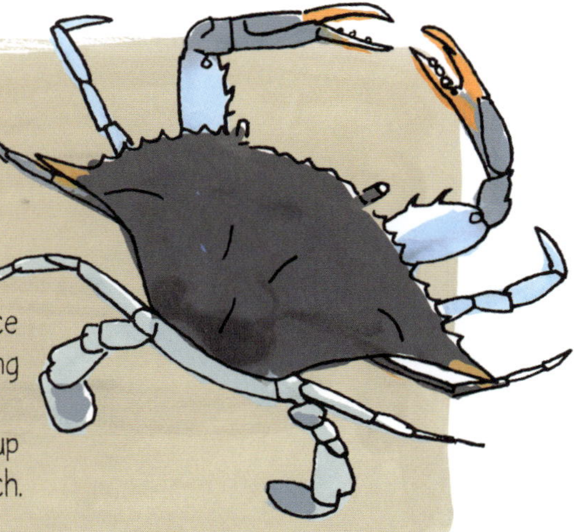

Females only mate once in their lifetimes, storing sperm for several subsequent broods of up to two million eggs each.

HERMIT CRAB

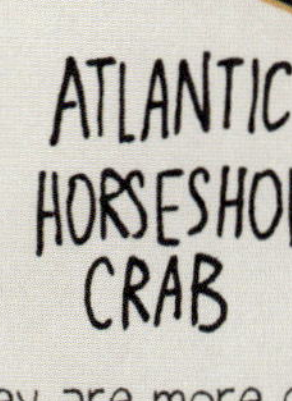

They must find a new shell as they grow and often take the shell of a bigger hermit crab that has vacated its shell for another.

ATLANTIC HORSESHOE CRAB

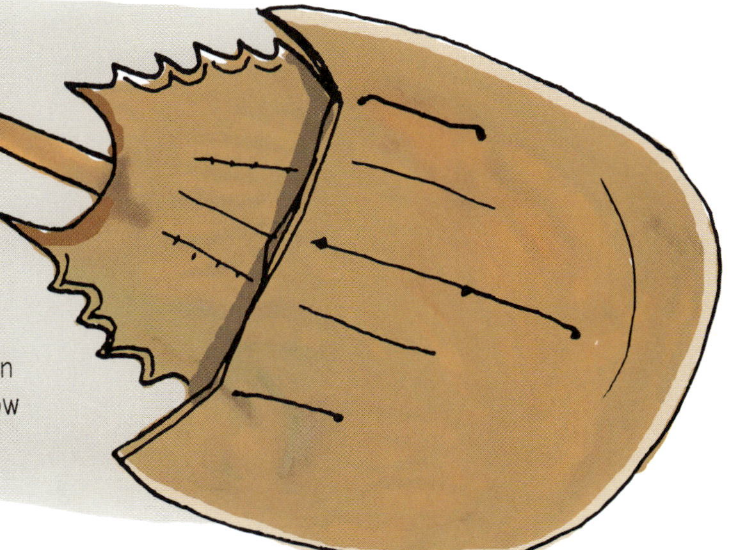

They are more closely related to arachnids like scorpions and spiders than true crabs and can regrow lost limbs.

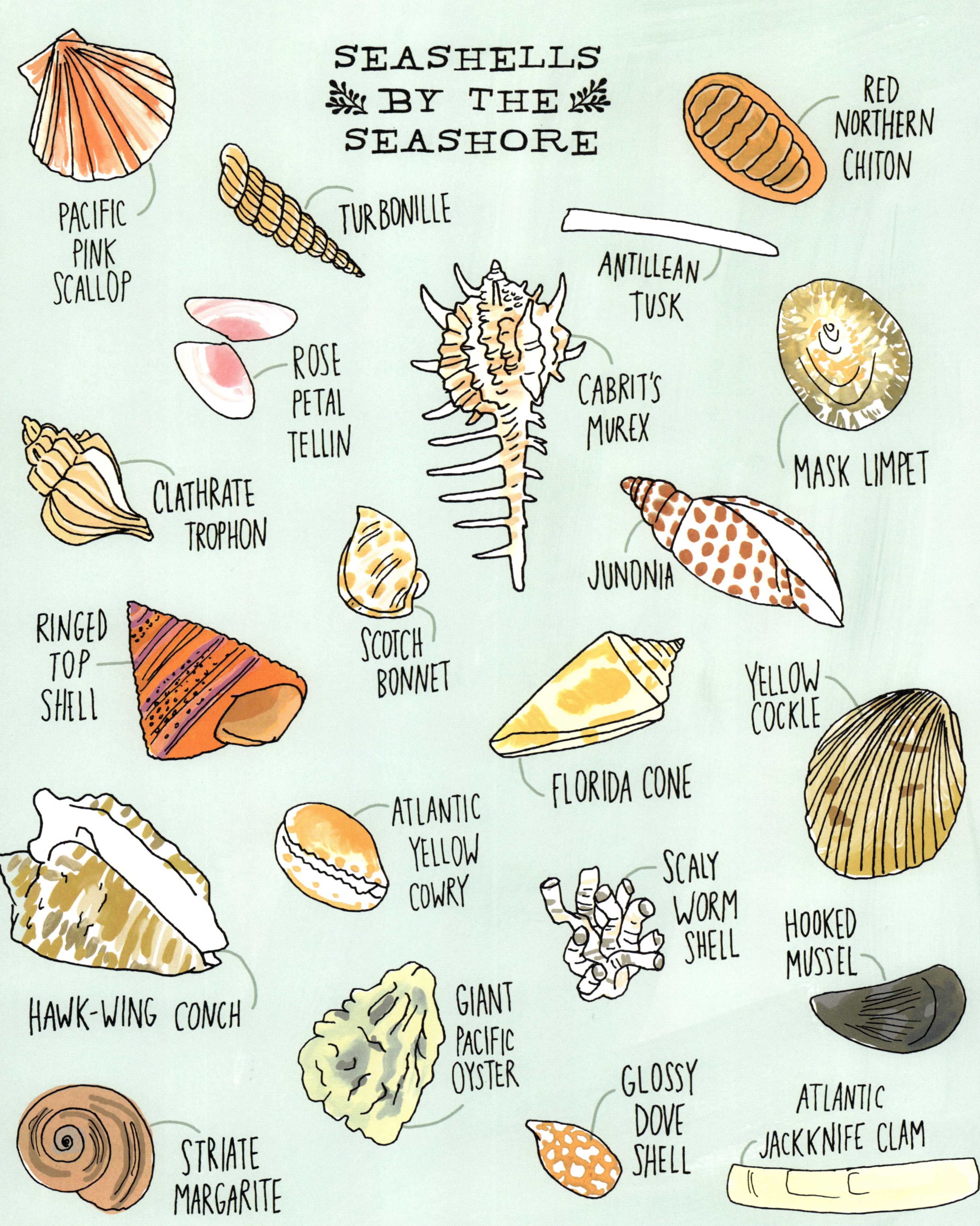

SEASHELLS BY THE SEASHORE
PACIFIC PINK SCALLOP
TURBONILLE
RED NORTHERN CHITON
ANTILLEAN TUSK
ROSE PETAL TELLIN
CABRIT'S MUREX
MASK LIMPET
CLATHRATE TROPHON
JUNONIA
RINGED TOP SHELL
SCOTCH BONNET
YELLOW COCKLE
FLORIDA CONE
ATLANTIC YELLOW COWRY
SCALY WORM SHELL
HOOKED MUSSEL
HAWK-WING CONCH
GIANT PACIFIC OYSTER
GLOSSY DOVE SHELL
ATLANTIC JACKKNIFE CLAM
STRIATE MARGARITE

SNOWFLAKES

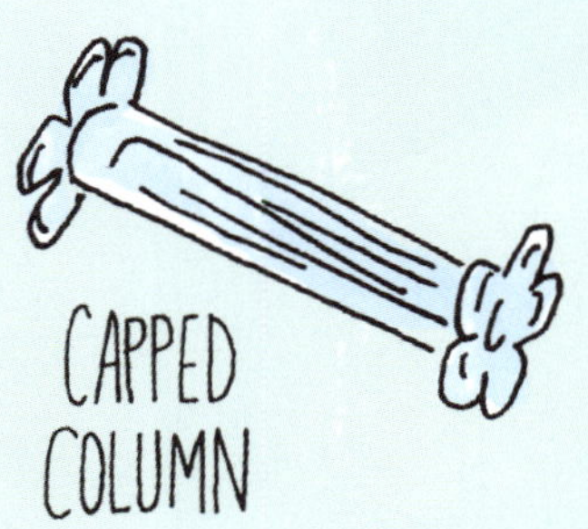

CAPPED COLUMN

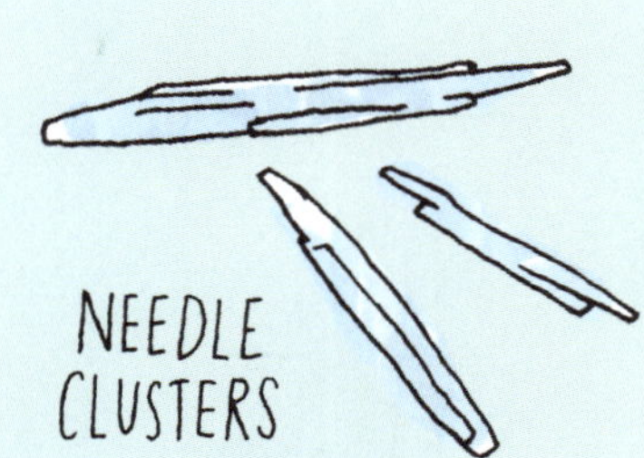

NEEDLE CLUSTERS

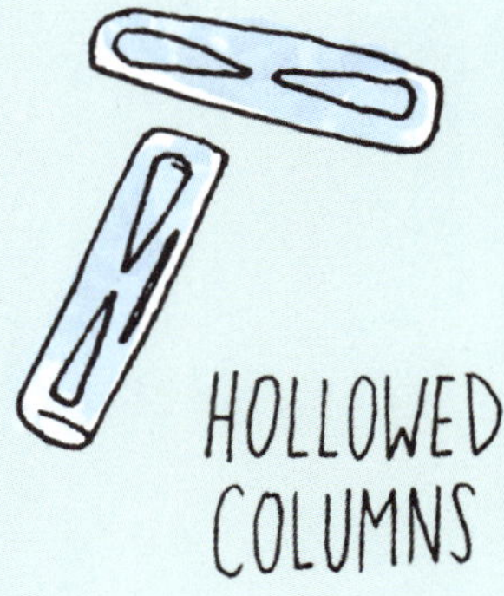

HOLLOWED COLUMNS

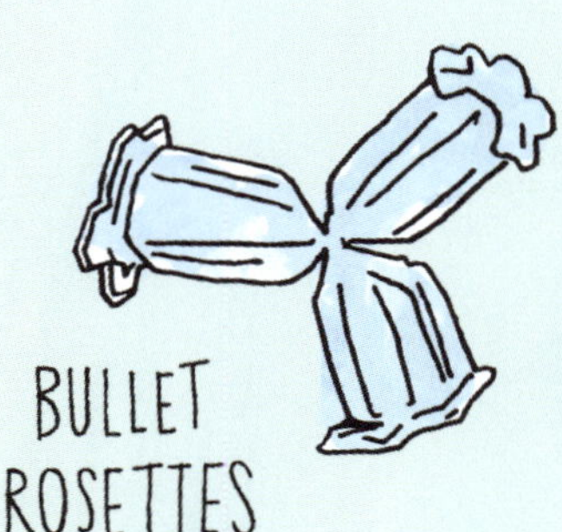

BULLET ROSETTES

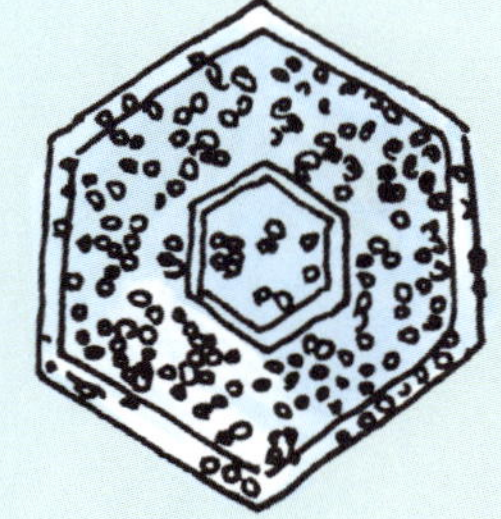

RIMED CRYSTAL

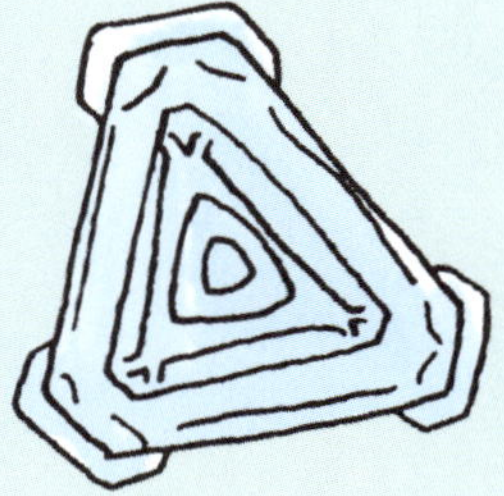

TRIANGULAR FORMS

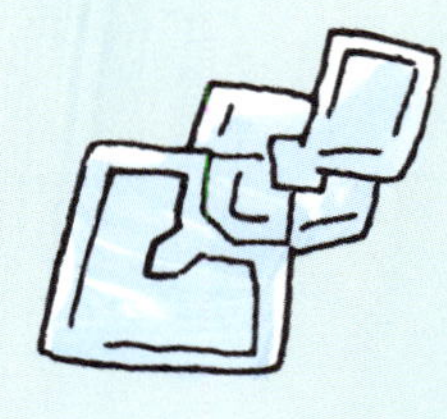

ARROWHEAD

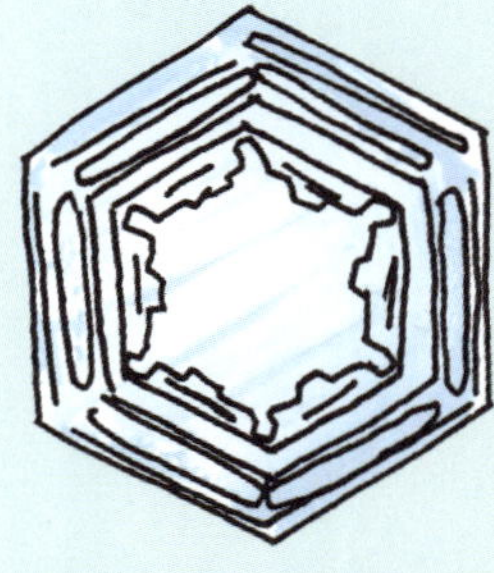

SIMPLE PRISM

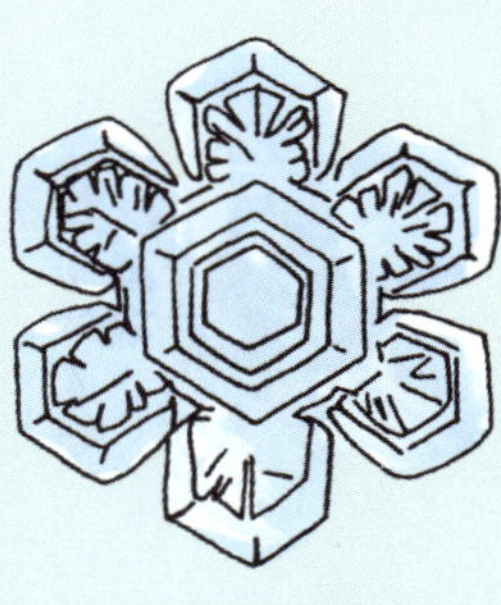

STELLAR PLATE

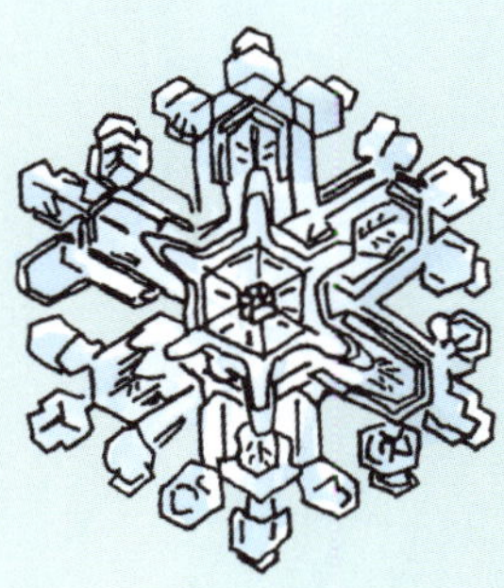

STELLAR DENDRITE

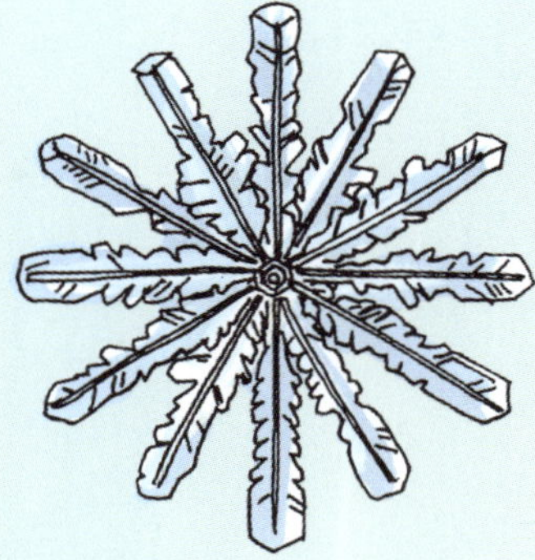

12-SIDED SNOWFLAKE

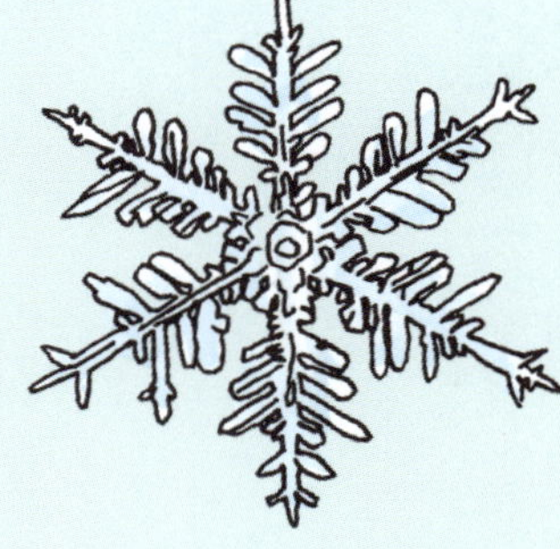

FERNLIKE STELLAR DENDRITE

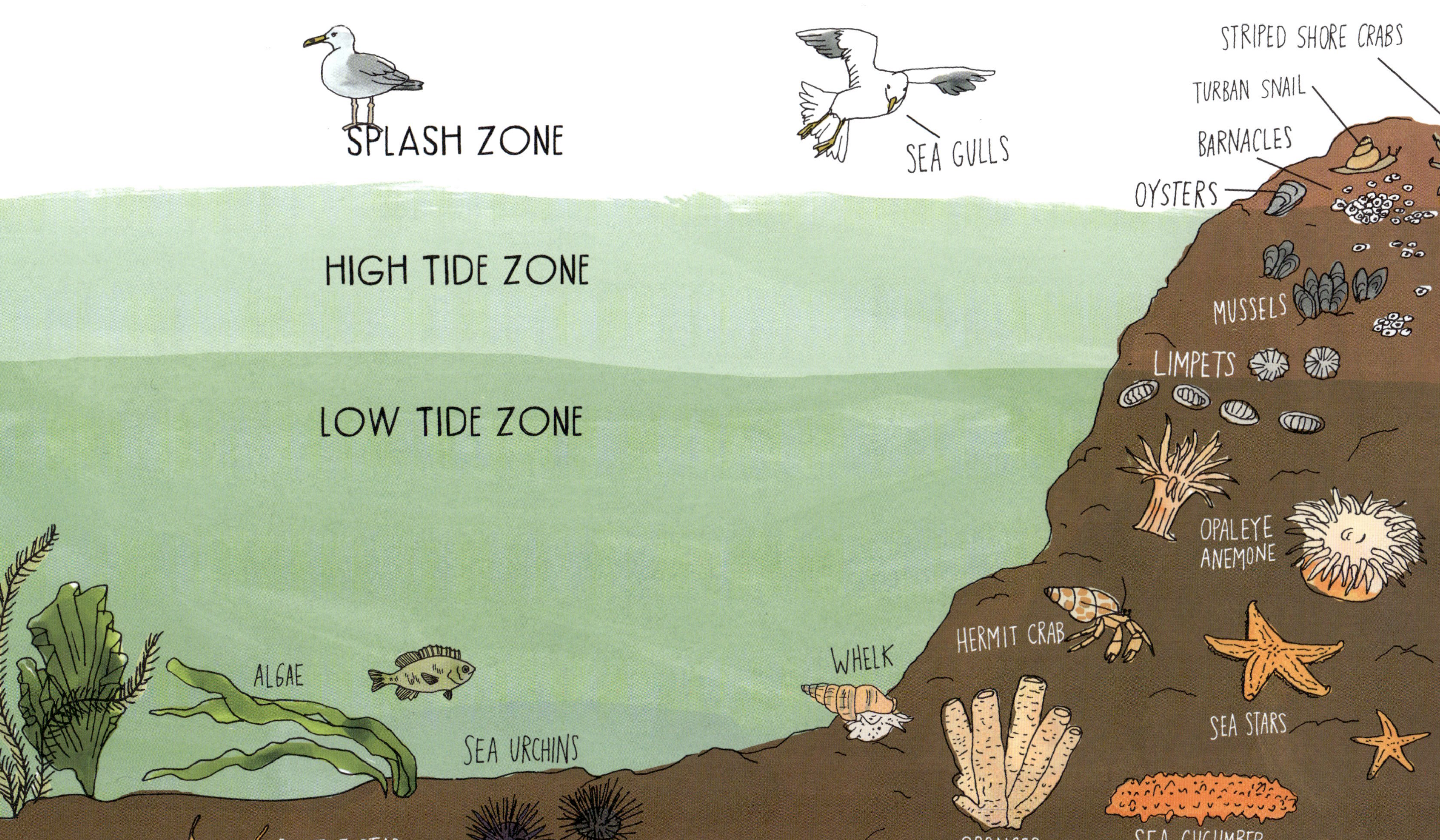

TIDAL ZONE ECOSYSTEM
SPLASH ZONE
SEA GULLS
STRIPED SHORE CRABS
TURBAN SNAIL
BARNACLES
OYSTERS
HIGH TIDE ZONE
MUSSELS
LIMPETS
OPALEYE ANEMONE
LOW TIDE ZONE
WHELK
HERMIT CRAB
SEA STARS
ALGAE
SEA URCHINS
SPONGES
SEA CUCUMBER
BRITTLE STAR

ANATOMY OF A DECIDUOUS TREE

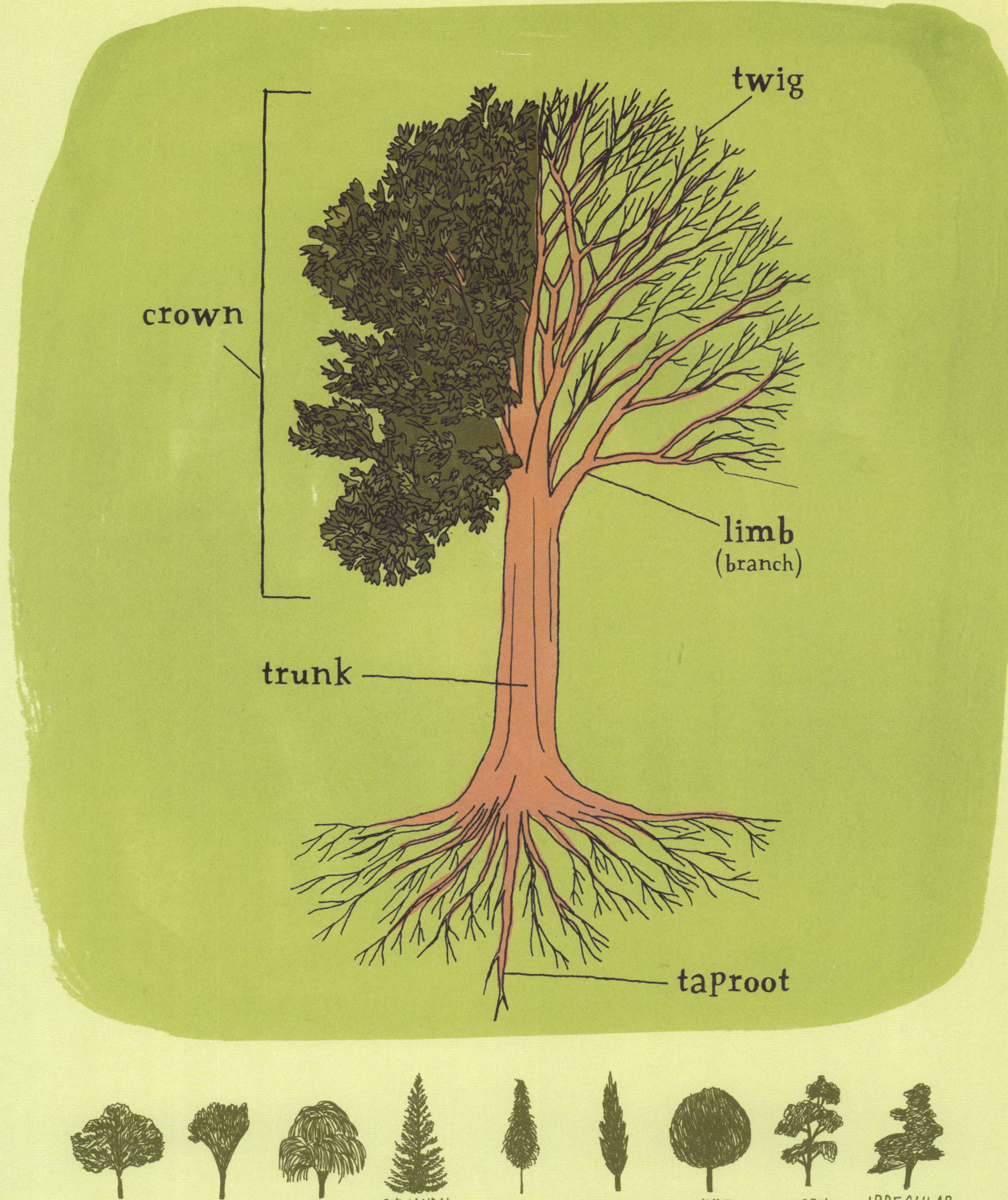